Gun Control

Gun Control

Look for these and other books in the Lucent Overview series:

Abortion
Acid Rain
Adoption
AIDS
Bigotry
Cancer
Censorship
Chemical Dependency
Cities
Civil Liberties
Cloning
Cults
The Death Penalty
Democracy
Divorce
Drug Abuse
Drugs and Sports
Drug Trafficking
Eating Disorders
Endangered Species
Environmental Groups
Epidemics
Espionage
Ethnic Violence
Euthanasia
Gambling
Gangs
Gay Rights
Hazardous Waste
Health Care

Homeless Children
Human Rights
Illegal Immigration
The Internet
Juvenile Crime
Medical Ethics
Mental Illness
Militias
Money
Obesity
Oil Spills
The Palestinian-Israeli Accord
Paranormal Phenomena
Police Brutality
Population
Poverty
Rap Music
The Rebuilding of Bosnia
Saving the American Wilderness
Schools
School Violence
Sexual Harassment
Smoking
Sports in America
Suicide
The U.S. Congress
The U.S. Presidency
Violence Against Women
Women's Rights
Zoos

Gun
Control

by L.K. Currie-McGhee

LUCENT
BOOKS®

THOMSON
GALE

San Diego • Detroit • New York • San Francisco • Cleveland • New Haven, Conn. • Waterville, Maine • London • Munich

LIBRARY OF CONGRESS CATALOGING-IN-PUBLICATION DATA

Currie-McGhee, L.K.
  Gun control / by L.K. Currie-McGhee.
    p. cm. — (Lucent overview series)
  Summary: Discusses issues surrounding the control of guns in America, such as the value of
  waiting periods, whether gun control prevents violence, and whether restrictions violate
  constitutional rights.
  Includes bibliographical references and index.
    ISBN 1-56006-658-X (alk. paper)
    1. Gun control—United States—Juvenile literature. [1. Gun control.] I. Title. II. Series.
  HV7436.C87 2004
  363.33'0973—dc22
                                                                              2003015026

Contents

Introduction

ON APRIL 20, 1999, Eric D. Harris, eighteen, and Dylan B. Klebold, seventeen, carried an arsenal of weapons into Columbine High School in Littleton, Colorado. With two sawed-off shotguns, a semiautomatic handgun, a semiautomatic carbine, and several homemade explosives, these two high school students ran rampant throughout the school, shooting at students and teachers alike.

Harris and Klebold killed thirteen people, including twelve of their classmates and one teacher. Then they killed themselves. Harris, Klebold, and all who died in the Columbine tragedy are among the nearly thirty thousand Americans who die from gun violence each year.

Where did they get their guns?

After the Columbine shooting, investigators discovered that the majority of the weapons the boys used originated from gun shows. Harris and Klebold bought the TEC-DC 19 semiautomatic handgun from twenty-two-year-old Mark Manes. Manes had legally obtained the gun at a gun show and then illegally sold it to Harris and Klebold, both under age eighteen at the time of the sale.

Harris and Klebold obtained the two sawed-off shotguns and the carbine with the help of their eighteen-year-old friend, Robyn Anderson. Anderson legally purchased the guns from gun show vendors and then gave the boys the weapons. She did not have to undergo a background check or provide any identification when she purchased the guns because she bought them from private dealers.

At the time, Colorado private dealers, people who sell firearms from their own collections, were not required to run background checks on purchasers at gun shows. "I would not have bought a gun for Eric or Dylan, if I had had to give any personal information or submit to any kind of check," Anderson recalled. "It was too easy. I wish it had been more difficult. Then I never would have helped them buy those guns."[1]

At a memorial service for the victims of the 1999 Columbine shooting, a mourner displays a sign pleading for gun control.

Do guns save lives?

A strikingly different incident involving firearms occurred several years prior when Sonya Dowdy went to the post office to pick up her mail and an armed man followed her back to her car. As Dowdy got into her car, the man lunged toward her before she could close the door. The man told her he was going to kill her and placed a .25 caliber pistol in her face.

Earlier that day, concerned for her safety, Dowdy's father had purchased a handgun and had given it to her. Dowdy quickly pulled out her gun and pointed it at her attacker. Seeing Dowdy's weapon, her attacker threw his gun down and ran

Advocates from both sides of the gun control issue clash in Washington, D.C. Discussions about gun control often turn into very heated debates.

away. The police later captured him. With her gun, Dowdy became one of the estimated hundreds of thousands to over a million Americans who annually use their guns to defend themselves from attackers.

Controversial debate

The Columbine and Dowdy examples are two of the many gun incidents discussed in America's gun control debate. The gun control debate is about whether or not stricter gun control laws—laws that regulate the manufacturing, sale, and ownership of firearms—should be enacted in the United States.

Although there are thousands of federal, state, and local gun laws already in place, some believe that tougher gun legislation is needed to combat gun violence. For example, in 1998 if all Colorado gun show vendors had been required to conduct background checks, Anderson may have been afraid to purchase the guns for Harris and Klebold. Without these weapons, it is possible that Harris and Klebold would not have been able to carry out their deadly shooting.

Critics of stricter gun legislation, often called gun rights advocates, charge that such laws would actually result in increased crime. Tougher gun laws could make it more difficult for law-abiding citizens to obtain guns, taking away their ability to defend themselves from attackers and burglaries. Sonya Dowdy, for example, may not have been able to obtain her gun and defend herself from her attacker if stricter firearm laws had been in place at the time of her assault.

Only two sides?

Gun control proponents believe that gun control laws would save more lives. Gun control opponents believe the same laws would take away lives. For this reason, the gun control debate is full of powerful emotion. People of opposing views on gun control often have a difficult time discussing gun control without it turning into a heated debate.

"The debate could hardly be more polarizing," writes Jonathan Cowan, president, and Jim Kessler, policy director, of Americans for Gun Safety, in 2001. "You're either pro-gun or anti-gun. You believe there is an individual right to own a gun or you don't. You draw the line at enforcing laws or you're for tough new gun-control laws. You believe crime and violence in America is all about a culture of violence or all about guns."[2]

Politicians, the media, gun control organizations, and gun rights organizations often portray the debate as one with only two choices. Americans are given the impression that they must choose to either support gun rights or gun control views, and that they cannot be proponents of both.

Middle ground

Despite this public portrayal of the debate, polls indicate that Americans believe there is room for middle ground between gun rights and gun control views. According to polls conducted by Americans for Gun Safety, the majority of Americans reject extremist views. Only 16 percent believe that gun ownership is an absolute right and only 9 percent believe that it is an absolute wrong.

Seventy percent of those polled stated that they believed that people have a right to own a gun, but that there was room for certain gun restrictions. Even 65 percent of gun owners polled who favorably viewed the National Rifle Association (NRA), a major proponent of gun rights, agreed that gun rights and gun restrictions could coexist.

Based on these polls, many Americans think it is time to change the terms of the gun control debate and come together to reduce gun violence. But in order to find middle ground, it is important to understand the debate as it exists today.

1

The Gun Culture in America

GUN OWNERSHIP HAS a long, established history in America. Although the gun control debate did not become a significant issue until the twentieth century, the origins of the American gun culture date back to when the colonists first stepped foot on American soil. From the beginning of colonial settlement, firearms were considered as essential as the ax and the plow.

After the colonies were established, Americans used firearms to protect newly settled land, to defend the United States during wars, and in a number of hunting and sporting activities. As guns became cheaper and more accessible, gun ownership grew more popular.

Today, approximately 40 percent of Americans own firearms. Because gun ownership and use was prevalent in American society from its inception and still is today, the United States is said to have a "gun culture." To many firearm owners, their guns are a symbol of America's freedom and way of life.

English inheritance

From the earliest development of firearms in the 1300s, people recognized the lethal ability and power of guns. Medieval European leaders soon realized that armed rebellious subjects could use the lethal power of guns against the government. To prevent uprisings, government authorities regulated who could own firearms.

American colonists used firearms to defend themselves from Native American attack.

In England, although the English Bill of Rights granted that its citizens could own and use firearms for their defense, gun ownership was conditional. Gun owners had to be gentlemen of the Protestant faith, because gentlemen—men in the wealthy, upper class of society—were considered less likely to rebel than commoners.

In 1607, when 105 English settlers established Jamestown, Virginia, the first permanent North American English colony, they continued to follow English gun laws. As a result, only the fifty-four gentlemen of Jamestown's settlers could own and shoot muskets. It was the gentlemen's responsibility to defend Jamestown from attacks by Native American tribes.

Limited gun ownership for commoners

The Jamestown colonists soon realized that they could better protect their community if all men were armed. Additionally, if all men owned rifles, every man could hunt for game and help feed the community. For these reasons, Jamestown authorities lifted the gun restrictions, allowing commoners to own firearms.

As more colonies were established, the new colonial governments followed Jamestown's example. Both commoners and gentlemen were not only allowed, but also encouraged to own guns for self-defense. The colonial governments formed militias to protect their settlements and often required that all healthy males enlist and each member be armed.

Although the colonial authorities allowed commoners to own guns, they also instituted strict legislation to prevent the "undesirable" from bearing firearms. Colonial leaders, whose communities were made up of predominantly white European Protestants, feared that armed African Americans, Native Americans, and Catholics would revolt against the local governments. As a result of this fear, colonial authorities passed several laws restricting who could own firearms. In 1642, Connecticut banned the sale of firearms or ammunition to Native Americans. Virginia, in 1648, passed the Act Preventing Negroes from Bearing Arms, which prohibited African Americans from owning firearms. In 1756, Connecticut authorities confiscated firearms from its Catholic population.

Birth of the Second Amendment

Authorities in England also worried about rebellious subjects and passed laws to disarm them. To the English, the American colonists were a potential threat. American settlers had grown frustrated with English taxes and were considering revolting. English leaders imposed an embargo on firearms and ammunition to the colonies.

Despite the embargo, the American colonists found ways to arm themselves. They imported 80 percent of their firearms and 90 percent of their gunpowder from Holland and France. With revolutionary zeal, the American colonists went to war in 1775 to win independence from England. Despite critical shortages of arms and ammunition, over the next eight years the Americans managed to arm the Continental army, local militias, and Native American allies and defeat the English. In 1783, England officially recognized the United States of America as an independent country.

The government of the United States was outlined in the Constitution, adopted by the states in 1787. A critical element of this document is the Bill of Rights, ten amendments to the Constitution guaranteeing basic personal freedoms. The Second Amendment deals with the issue of individual citizens bearing arms and states keeping militias. Although its meaning is debated today, the Second Amendment's immediate results were that individual gun ownership was unrestricted and states could maintain armed militias, separate from the federal government's army.

During the Revolutionary War, American colonists like these ignored the firearm embargo and imported guns to use against the British.

Gun culture emerges

In the years following the Revolutionary War, the U.S. government armed the state militias and the standing army by purchasing guns from both foreign and domestic gun manufacturers. During the Mexican War, fought from 1846 to 1848, the U.S. government stepped up its domestic gun purchases, offering more contracts to U.S. manufacturers, such as Samuel Colt.

After the Mexican War, U.S. gun manufacturers focused on selling to private citizens. Colt marketed to civilians through traveling salesmen, advertising, and gun shows. In 1855, Colt built the largest private armory in the world in order to fulfill demand.

The Civil War erupted in 1861 and temporarily interrupted civilian gun sales. During the Civil War, from 1861 to 1865, American gun manufacturers were mostly based in the North. They furnished the Union army with the majority of the estimated 4 million small arms it used.

The Confederate army was forced to rely on European manufacturers, importing approximately two hundred thousand weapons. After the war, the Union army allowed its soldiers to take their government-issued guns home. The federal government also let many of the defeated Confederate soldiers keep their pistols, although the soldiers had to turn in their rifles. As a result, thousands of veterans returned to civilian life owning guns.

The wild west

By the middle of the nineteenth century, the United States had gained an image as a gun-toting society and was known for a culture where guns were seen as a necessary part of society. The birth of the Wild West added to this image. When Americans moved westward, the federal government sold surplus rifles, pistols, and ammunition to the westward-bound emigrants so that they could defend themselves and their land primarily from Native Americans.

The West became known as lawless country where pioneers took justice into their own hands using their Colt six-shooters and Winchester rifles. The Western frontiersmen sometimes resorted to using guns to settle disputes. Answering a question about how many men he had shot and killed, "Wild Bill" Hickok, a gun-toting lawman, boasted that with his pistol, "I suppose I have killed considerably more than a hundred . . . [and not] one without good cause."[3]

Although Hickok's claim was believed to be an exaggeration, people clamored to read about his and other Western gunslingers' exploits. Men such as Hickok were portrayed as heroes, despite the fact that their claim to fame was violence. Magazine writers and dime novelists glorified the gunslingers, praising their shooting ability. Being able to shoot straight was considered a necessary skill for defending oneself against Native Americans and other gunslingers. As a result, frontier boys were taught to shoot at an early age, in preparation of defending their land and themselves.

National Rifle Association

As gun ownership continued to flourish, shooting contests and gun clubs became popular outlets for recreational gun use. The National Rifle Association, or NRA, a nationwide gun club, was established in 1871 by Civil War veterans Colonel William C. Church and Captain George Wingate. They had been upset by the lack of marksmanship in their men and created the National Rifle Association as a nonprofit organization to promote better shooting skills.

The NRA helped found rifle clubs and sponsored nationwide target-shooting contests. Additionally, the organization established a relationship with the U.S. government and enjoyed perks such as buying surplus rifles and ammunition from the government at bargain prices. The NRA would grow to be the largest organization of American gun owners, a major lobbyist against gun control initiatives, and a powerful voice in the gun control debate.

Gun violence escalates

As guns proliferated during the nineteenth century, so did their role in violent crime. According to Alexander DeConde, author of *Gun Violence in America,* "In the post–Civil War

years, firearms became more acceptable, more lethal and subject to a greater willingness by Americans to use them in homicides than in the past."[4] Before 1846, guns were used in 17 percent of homicides; by the end of the nineteenth century, that number had risen to 47 percent.

Concerned with the growing violence, state governments made attempts to control gun use as early as 1813, when Kentucky passed a weapons control law aimed at restricting the carrying of concealed weapons. By 1850, several other states had enacted similar laws and some towns passed local ordinances banning weapons within city limits. Despite these restrictions, violence continued to spread.

The exploits of gun-toting cowboys like these gave rise to the image of the West as a place of extreme violence.

By the early twentieth century, major U.S. cities were seeing a surge of armed crimes, and more states passed laws to combat firearm violence. For example, New York passed the Sullivan Law in 1911, which required people to obtain a license to legally possess a handgun. The NRA denounced the Sullivan Law and other early gun control legislation, arguing that these laws made it difficult for law-abiding citizens to obtain firearms. In 1911, James Drain, the NRA president, addressed the Sullivan Law in the magazine *Arms and the Man.* Drain wrote, "A warning should be sounded to legislators against passing laws which . . . seem to make it impossible for a criminal to get a pistol, if the same laws would make it very difficult for an honest man and good citizen to obtain them."[5] Despite the NRA's argument, as Americans faced increasing gun violence, many supported tough gun legislation.

The first federal gun laws

Criminal activity involving firearms grew in the 1920s in connection with the illegal manufacturing and sales of liquor

The emergence of gangsters and the growth of organized crime during the 1920s and 1930s led to an increase in gun violence.

during Prohibition. Rival gangs often clashed using submachine guns during their violent encounters. Their shooting sprees shocked the public and fueled the belief that society was becoming lawless.

The public's fears escalated in the 1930s as gangsters' exploits made headlines across the country. Violent crime rates rose by 50 percent over the previous decade. Gangsters such as John Dillinger and "Pretty Boy" Floyd engaged in gun battles where federal agents and innocent bystanders were shot and killed with submachine guns. Scared and outraged, citizens pressured the government to pass a federal law, a law that applies nationwide restricting firearm availability. Americans wanted a federal law because state and local gun laws were not consistent across the country. For example, in 1934, only a few states, such as Arkansas, required that people obtain a permit before purchasing a handgun.

Congress responded by passing the National Firearms Act in 1934. This law made it difficult for Americans to purchase submachine guns and sawed-off shotguns, both of which were common in criminal activity, by applying a high-priced tax on these weapons. Four years later, Congress passed the Federal Firearms Act, which required gun dealers to obtain federal licenses and maintain sales records, giving the government the ability to monitor gun transactions. This law also banned selling firearms to felons, but because gun dealers had no way to investigate a purchaser's background, felons could lie about their history and still obtain a gun.

After these laws passed, America's attention turned from domestic gun violence to the global conflict of World War II, which lasted from 1939 to 1945. It was not until the high-profile shootings and widespread social unrest in the 1960s that gun violence was brought to the forefront once again.

The growing gun control movement

The 1960s were marked by civil rights and anti–Vietnam War protest and more high-profile gun violence, including the 1963 assassination of President John F. Kennedy and the 1968 assassinations of civil rights leader Dr. Martin Luther King Jr. and U.S. senator Robert Kennedy. These shootings touched off another public outcry for federal gun legislation. Congress responded by passing the Gun Control Act of 1968. This law forbade gun purchases through the mail and prohibited dealers from selling guns to people such as the mentally ill and drug abusers. Although gun control proponents supported this law, they believed that stricter gun laws, such as gun registration, where gun owners must register their guns with the government, were still needed.

To achieve their goals, gun control advocates banded together in national organizations. In 1974, Mark Borinsky, a victim of a robbery at gunpoint, founded the first national gun control organization, the National Council to Control Handguns, later renamed Handgun Control, Inc. (HCI), which would grow to 750,000 members by the year 2001. Initially the organization's goal was to ban handguns in the United States, but the group soon adopted a more moderate mission of supporting the enactment and enforcement of gun control laws that they claimed would ensure only law-abiding citizens could purchase guns.

Brady campaign to prevent gun violence

In 1981, a highly publicized, tragic gun incident again shocked the nation, spurring more citizens to join gun control organizations. A disturbed man from Colorado, John W. Hinckley Jr., used a .22 caliber revolver with exploding head bullets—one of a collection of firearms he had purchased legally despite a history of psychiatric problems—to attempt to assassinate President Ronald Reagan. President Reagan was wounded but fully recovered from the shooting. White House press secretary James Brady was shot in the head, paralyzing him for life. This prompted James Brady and his wife Sarah to become gun control supporters.

Four years later, another gun incident turned Sarah Brady from a supporter into HCI's most well-known activist. Sarah Brady and her six-year-old son climbed into a friend's pickup truck, where Brady's son picked up a gun he had found on the seat. Both she and her son thought the gun was a toy. "I took it from him and realized it was a fully loaded little .22," Sarah Brady recalls. "I just kind of went crazy. How could

anybody leave a gun where a child could find it?"[6] Sarah Brady reacted by joining HCI to fight for gun regulations such as laws requiring adults to store their guns in places inaccessible to children. She went on to become HCI's chairperson in 1989, and twelve years later HCI was renamed the Brady Campaign to Prevent Gun Violence, in honor of James and Sarah Brady.

Chaos reigned on this Washington, D.C., sidewalk just moments after John Hinckley Jr. shot Ronald Reagan and James Brady in 1981.

Federal gun control legislation

By 1985, HCI had grown to more than 275,000 members, enabling the organization to step up its gun control efforts. Through letter campaigns and HCI-funded advertisements, HCI helped persuade Congress to pass the Law Enforcement Officers' Protection Act in 1986 and the Undetectable Firearms Act in 1988.

The Law Enforcement Officers' Protection Act bans armor-piercing, "cop-killer" bullets, reducing the chance that criminals can obtain ammunition capable of puncturing police officers' bulletproof vests. The Undetectable Firearms Act outlaws guns that cannot be detected in an airport metal detector, preventing people from boarding an airplane with a gun. Buoyed by the success of these acts, HCI pressed for Congress to pass the so-called Brady Bill, which would require gun dealers to perform background checks on gun purchasers.

The "gun lobby," made up of the NRA and fellow gun rights organizations, managed to initially block the Brady Bill, but as gun violence continued to escalate, more Americans pressed for mandatory background checks. By 1993, when gun violence reached an all-time peak with 39,595 American firearm-related deaths for that year, a Gallup Poll indicated that 88 percent of citizens supported the Brady Bill. Responding to public support and strong backing by President Bill Clinton, Congress passed the Brady Handgun Violence Prevention Act, named in honor of James Brady, in 1993.

The passed act became known as the Brady law. This law requires that federally licensed dealers check rifle and handgun purchasers' backgrounds before selling to them. If a dealer discovers that a customer is a prohibited gun purchaser, such as a convicted felon, the dealer cannot sell firearms to the purchaser.

Gun rights reactions

All along, the gun lobby has argued that in addition to being ineffective, American gun control laws are the beginning of a slippery slope and, if not stopped, will lead to the confiscation of guns from law-abiding citizens. "[It] is kind of like the old Bert Laher commercial that used to be on television," NRA chief Harlon Carter testified to Congress in 1975 as he discussed the Bureau of Alcohol, Tobacco, Firearms and Explosives (ATF) request for fourteen-day waiting periods. "He used to eat a potato chip and say 'I'll bet you can't eat just one.'"[7] Carter believed that approval of the waiting periods would lead to an onslaught of gun regulations.

Beginning in the 1970s, the NRA aggressively countered the growing gun control movement. In 1975, the NRA established the Institute for Legislative Action (ILA), a lobbying division that applies political pressure by methods such as donating funds to legislators who oppose gun control. Additionally, throughout the 1980s, the NRA placed ads featuring NRA members, both celebrities and everyday individuals, in magazines such as *Southern Living* to attract people from all backgrounds. As a result, the NRA grew to more than 2 million members by 1983.

With the ILA's efforts and members' letter campaigns, the NRA was able to lobby Congress to pass the Firearm Owners Protection Act in 1986. This law relaxed gun and ammunition restrictions by dropping the ban on selling guns across state lines and allowing persons who committed nonviolent felonies to own firearms. The NRA followed up this success by persuading Congress to defeat several proposed gun control laws, including one requiring waiting periods before citizens could purchase a gun.

James Brady looks on as President Bill Clinton signs the Brady law requiring background checks for gun purchases.

Despite its achievements, the NRA believes that current gun legislation is too restrictive. For example, the NRA is working to repeal certain state laws that ban citizens from carrying concealed weapons, arguing that allowing citizens to carry concealed firearms deters criminals from committing crimes. In contrast, the Brady Campaign to Prevent Gun Violence believes that today's gun laws are not strict enough and lobbies for stronger gun legislation, such as a law that would require private sellers to run background checks on purchasers at gun shows.

The controversy continues

Current events have provided arguments for each side of the gun control debate. In the late 1990s, more than fifteen tragic school shootings in the United States shocked communities and made headlines around the world. In reaction to the shootings, American mothers united to fight for stronger gun control laws. On Mother's Day 2000, over 750,000 people participated in the Million Mom March on the Mall in

The NRA and other gun lobbyists believe that current gun control laws are too restrictive and punish law-abiding gun owners like this woman.

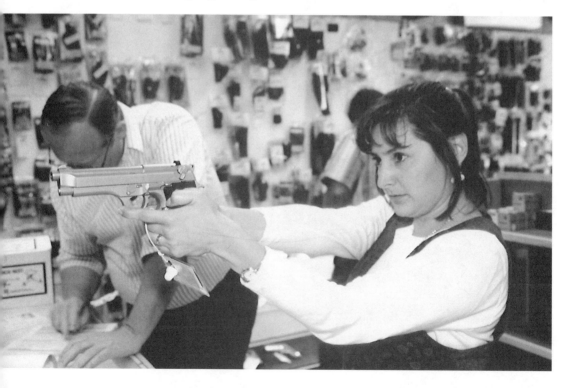

Washington, D.C. Their goal was to persuade lawmakers to support strict enforcement of existing gun control laws and new initiatives such as requiring safety locks on guns.

In 2002, another highly publicized incident prompted calls for new gun laws. Snipers shot thirteen people, ten fatally, in the Washington, D.C., region while eluding an intense manhunt for twenty-one days. Gun control proponents claim that a national ballistic fingerprint database, a database that would track unique markings that guns leave on fired bullets, would have helped federal agents trace the bullets back to the weapon and the snipers, John Allen Muhammed and John Lee Malvo. Gun rights advocates heatedly dispute this claim.

In contrast, the tragedy of September 11, 2001—when terrorists flew hijacked planes into the World Trade Center in New York City, the Pentagon in Washington, D.C., and a field in Pennsylvania—prompted a surge of support in America for self-defense programs and gun ownership. James Jay Baker, former NRA Institute for Legislative Action executive director, gave his reason for this surge during his speech at the 2002 NRA annual meeting. "When ordinary citizens saw for themselves the ferocity of modern-day terrorism, they lined up . . . at gun store counters to reach for America's original homeland security—the Second Amendment."[8]

In the year following the tragedy, gun sales rose across the United States. For example, Connecticut gun sales increased nearly 9 percent and Pennsylvania gun purchases rose 8 percent. Based on the increasing number of Americans buying guns, it is evident that the United States still has a strong gun culture and many citizens believe that gun ownership is necessary to preserve their rights and freedom. For this reason, gun control is often met with resistance, resulting in a polarized national debate.

2

Second Amendment Interpretations

A WELL-REGULATED militia, being necessary to the security of a free State, the right of the people to keep and bear arms, shall not be infringed.– Second Amendment, U.S. Constitution

Irreconcilable interpretations of the Second Amendment lie at the heart of the gun control debate. One of these is the "individual rights" interpretation, which states that the Second Amendment gives individual citizens the right to own and use firearms for their own defense. Another, the "collective rights" interpretation, is that the Second Amendment protects the collective right of states to maintain armed militias in order to defend the states and the nation. Based on this viewpoint, the Second Amendment does not protect an individual's right to defend himself with firearms.

These interpretations are important because they are used in the current gun control debate to support each side's opposing positions. Gun rights proponents believe that the individual rights interpretation of the Second Amendment is the correct one. Using this theory, they claim that gun control laws violate Americans' constitutional right to bear arms. Gun control advocates support the collective rights interpretation of the Second Amendment, using it to back up their claim that gun control laws do not violate individuals' Second Amendment rights.

Second Amendment origins

Both supporters of the collective rights interpretation and the individual rights interpretation use the Second Amendment's wording and history to support their viewpoints. The origins of the Second Amendment date back to the 1787 constitutional convention. During this convention, U.S. legislators debated about whether the United States should be an association of allied, but independent states, or a single country with one ruling government.

Members of the Federalist political party believed that the United States should be a single country with a strong central government and that there should be a national standing army to protect the country. James Madison, a Federalist, presented the proposed U.S. Constitution at the convention which called for these things.

Anti-Federalist legislators criticized the proposed Constitution. They believed that a strong federal government would be too powerful and could become corrupt. Specifically, they feared that with a national army, the central government could easily revoke Americans' hard-earned freedoms.

The Anti-Federalists preferred that the states retain more power than the proposed Constitution called for, in order to keep the federal government in check. They would not support the Constitution unless there was a counterweight to the standing army. Noah Webster, a Federalist, supported the Anti-Federalists' view that a counterweight was needed. "Before a standing army can rule, the people must be disarmed; as they are in almost every kingdom in Europe," Webster explained. "The supreme power in America cannot enforce unjust laws by the sword; because the whole body of people are armed and constitute a force superior to any band of regular troops that can be, on any pretence, raised by the United States."[9] Webster

Noah Webster insisted that the Constitution include a provision allowing citizens to bear arms.

believed that allowing citizens to keep their arms would be an effective counter to the standing army, giving Americans the ability to protect their freedoms.

A compromise

In order to gain the Anti-Federalists' support for the Constitution, James Madison promised that after ratification of the Constitution, he would ask Congress to amend the Constitution with wording that would protect personal freedoms. By June 8, 1789, the Constitution was ratified by all thirteen states. Madison then fulfilled his promise to the Anti-Federalists. After the Constitution's ratification he proposed that the Bill of Rights, which included the Second Amendment, be added to the Constitution.

The draft Second Amendment that Madison presented to Congress stated, "The right of the people to keep and bear arms shall not be infringed; a well armed and well regulated militia being the best security of a free country; but no person religiously scrupulous of bearing arms shall be compelled to render military service in person."[10] Before approval, Congress changed the draft Second Amendment in order to suit the majority of the congressional representatives.

Congress dropped the phrase about religiously scrupulous people from the draft Second Amendment because they believed that including it would give the government the ability to declare people religiously scrupulous and then exclude them from service. Additionally, Congress struck the phrase "well armed" from the amendment because legislators felt that "well regulated" implied well armed.

After the changes, the Second Amendment received congressional approval. Following this approval, the Bill of Rights was sent to the states. During the next two years, the states approved ten of the Bill of Rights' twelve proposed amendments, including the Second Amendment. With the ratification of the Bill of Rights, both the Federalists and Anti-Federalists were satisfied.

The Federalists had gained a strong central government through the Constitution and the Anti-Federalists had secured

amendments that would protect citizens' personal freedoms. Additionally, the states could maintain armed militias, which the Anti-Federalists believed would prevent tyranny by the federal government. However, although the Second Amendment was part of a compromise between the Federalists and Anti-Federalists, it would become a major source of controversy in the twentieth century.

Second Amendment intent

When gun violence escalated in the early 1900s, so did calls for gun control laws. As the calls grew louder, opponents of gun control legislation also became vocal, arguing against such laws. Each side of the gun control debate began to use opposing interpretations of the Second Amendment to defend their positions. Since that time, the Second Amendment has been an integral part of the gun control debate.

Because there are no known records that specifically define what the founders intended the Second Amendment to mean, it is open to interpretation. Still, Americans use different supporting evidence to back their contrasting interpretations. Many turn to what may have influenced James Madison when he drafted the Second Amendment.

One possibility is that Madison based the Second Amendment on a provision in the English Bill of Rights, which states that individuals may possess arms to defend themselves, although this right is limited to Protestants. If Madison wrote the Second Amendment in the same spirit of the English Bill of Rights, then he likely intended to give individuals the right to bear arms. The fact that early American leaders often emulated the English legal framework, customs and laws support the position that the Second Amendment was based on the English Bill of Rights provision.

Virginia's influence

Another possibility is that Madison based the Second Amendment on a militia provision found in Virginia's Declaration of Rights. Virginia's Declaration of Rights, written in 1776, states:

> A well regulated militia, composed of the body of the people, trained to arms, is the proper, natural, and safe defense of a free state; that standing armies, in time of peace, should be avoided as dangerous to liberty; and that, in all cases, the military should be under strict subordination to, and be governed by, the civil power.[11]

This provision provides the right to bear arms to members of Virginia's militia, not to all individual citizens. If Madison based the Second Amendment on this provision, then it is likely that he meant for the Second Amendment to only protect the states' collective rights to maintain militias.

Madison was a Virginian politician, which supports the possibility that Madison based the Second Amendment on the Virginia provision. Additionally, certain phrases in the Second Amendment are similar to those in the Virginia provision. However, documentation has not conclusively supported what specifically influenced Madison when he wrote the Bill of Rights, so Americans continue to debate about the possibilities.

The people

In addition to debating about Second Amendment influences, Americans also debate about the specific meaning of each word in the Second Amendment. Most of the key phrases can be interpreted differently based on their context in the amendment and how the phrase was used historically. For example, "the people" is interpreted in two different ways.

One view is that "the people" refers to all people in the United States. If the term "the people" means everybody, then the Second Amendment gives all Americans the right to bear arms. This supports the individual rights interpretation of the Second Amendment.

Another interpretation of "the people" is that the phrase only applies to militia members. This is based on the phrase's placement in the amendment. "The people" is preceded by the phrase "a well regulated militia, being necessary to the security of a free State." The founding fathers may have placed the militia phrase before "the people" in order to show that the amendment only referred to people in militias. Supporters of the collective rights interpretation of the Second Amendment are proponents of this definition.

Militia: selective or universal?

The word militia is also interpreted differently. One interpretation is that militias in colonial days were universal, meaning that all males were considered militia members. If militias were universal, then the Second Amendment's use of "militia" implies all men.

This definition lends support to the belief that the Second Amendment gives all people the right to bear arms. Proponents of this opinion cite quotes from early America's legislators to support their position. "Who are the militia?" colonial leader George Mason asked at a Virginia convention in 1788. "They consist now of the whole people."[12]

Those supporting the collective rights interpretation of the Second Amendment argue that militias of early America were not universal. They claim that state militias limited their members. For example, African Americans and Native Americans

The Second Amendment guaranteed militiamen like these the right to bear arms but did not specify whether this right extended to the larger populace.

were banned from serving in state militias. Based on these facts, they claim that "militia" referred to select men, which means that the Second Amendment applies only to people in militias and not all Americans.

To the courts

Americans have turned to the courts to interpret the Second Amendment. However, the courts have given conflicting rulings concerning the Second Amendment. As a result, both sides of the gun control debate are able to cite different rulings to support their opposing positions.

For example, the 1905 *City of Salina v. Blakesly* ruling from the Kansas Supreme Court supports the collective rights interpretation of the Second Amendment. Blakesly was convicted of carrying a pistol in the city of Salina while he was under the influence of alcohol.

The supreme court of Kansas ruled that the right to possess and carry a handgun is not absolute and that Blakesly did not have the right to carry a firearm throughout the city while under the influence. The Kansas court stated that the right to bear arms referred to a collective body, not individuals, and concluded that the right was intended for the defense of the country.

Presser v. Illinois

In contrast, the court ruling in *Presser v. Illinois* supports the individual rights interpretation of the Second Amendment. In 1886, Herman Presser was in charge of a German American private paramilitary shooting organization. Presser led a parade of four hundred armed men through the streets of Chicago without a permit. State authorities arrested him for violating an Illinois statute that prohibited drilling or parading without a license from the governor.

Presser eventually appealed to the U.S. Supreme Court, the highest court in the United States, claiming that the state violated his Second Amendment rights because he and his men had the right to walk through the streets with their firearms. The Supreme Court concluded that the state did not infringe on Presser's Second Amendment rights and upheld his conviction. The Supreme Court ruled that Presser's Second Amendment rights had not been violated because the Illinois statute did not prohibit Presser from keeping and bearing arms; it only kept him from parading without a license.

Second Amendment individual rights interpretation supporters claim that this case supports their position. Although the Supreme Court ruled against Presser, it also recognized that the Second Amendment did give Presser the right to own and use a firearm. The Court only ruled against him because the statute did not violate his Second Amendment right.

United States v. Cruikshank

Americans on both sides of the gun control debate also cite many of the same court cases to support their opposing interpretations of the Second Amendment. For example, the ruling of *United States v. Cruikshank,* a case that dealt with whether or not state gun laws were constitutional, can be inter-preted to support either the collective rights or individual rights interpretations of the Second Amendment.

In 1874, *United States v. Cruikshank* became the first major federal case concerning the Second Amendment to be heard by the Supreme Court. A ruling from the Supreme Court is a final ruling on a case and cannot be appealed. Provided it gives a clear decision about an issue, the ruling sets a precedent for future rulings on the same subject.

United States v. Cruikshank came about because of events that occurred on September 14, 1874. On this day, several thousand members of the White League, an anti–African American group, clashed with five hundred police and black militia members in Colfax, Louisiana. The police and black militia were attempting to defend the city from being taken over by the White League.

The White League disarmed the militia and temporarily seized control. As a result, twenty-seven people died during

the clash. William J. Cruikshank was one of the leaders of the White League and he, along with ninety-five others, was charged with preventing black citizens from exercising their right to bear arms.

Different interpretations

The Court ruled that Cruikshank and the other defendants did not violate the black militia members' right to bear arms. It held that the Second Amendment only protects the people's right to bear arms from actions by the federal government and not from citizens or states. Based on this ruling, it can be inferred that the Court believed that the federal government could not infringe on citizens' right to bear arms, but state governments and individuals, if they desired, could impose gun control legislation on their citizens.

However, the Court also stated that the right to bear arms was not dependent on the Constitution for its existence. Based on this statement, many contend that the Court recognized that the right of the people to bear arms as a natural right, preceding the Constitution. Additionally, the Court stated that a militia consisted of all citizens able to bear arms. This supports the theory that militias were considered to be universal. Therefore, the Second Amendment applies to all people.

Proponents of gun control use this case to support their stance that the states can impose gun control laws. Gun rights advocates use this case to support their belief that the right to bear arms is a natural right of all people and that gun control laws violate this right.

United States v. Miller

United States v. Miller, another Second Amendment case, reached the U.S. Supreme Court in 1939. While the *United States v. Cruikshank* ruling deals with the constitutionality of state gun control laws, the *United States v. Miller* ruling concerns the constitutionality of federal gun laws. Like *United States v. Cruikshank, United States v. Miller* can be interpreted in different ways.

In the 1939 case, the defendants, Jack Miller and Frank Layton, were charged with violating the National Firearms

Act (NFA) because they had transported an unregistered short-barreled shotgun from Oklahoma to Arkansas. The men pleaded that the NFA, a federal law that requires the registration of weapons such as theirs, improperly used federal power to control firearms, violating their Second Amendment rights.

The Arkansas district court agreed with Miller and Layton and its judge dismissed the charges against them. Federal attorneys appealed to the Supreme Court. The Supreme Court reversed the lower court's ruling and confirmed the constitutionality of the NFA. Because the NFA, a federal gun control law, was ruled to be constitutional, many interpret this case to mean that the Second Amendment allows for federal gun control laws.

However, the Court also made statements that supported the individual rights interpretation of the Second Amendment. The Court stated that the entire populace constituted a militia. Additionally, the Court stated that the Second Amendment protects the right of an individual to keep and bear militia-type arms. Many contend that the Court ruled against Miller and Layton only because it lacked evidence showing that Miller and Layton's weapon had a militia purpose.

United States v. Emerson

Even current Second Amendment cases are used in the debate about the Second Amendment and gun control. Recently, *United States v. Emerson* reached the Fifth Circuit Court of Appeals. In this case, Timothy Emerson, a doctor from San Angelo, Texas, stood trial for possessing a firearm while under a court-issued protective order during his 1998 divorce; the order was issued because Emerson was considered a potential domestic violence threat. Federal law prohibits parties subject to a protective order from owning guns.

The court upheld the federal and state gun laws that disarmed Emerson because he was a domestic violence threat. This ruling can be used to support the constitutionality of gun control laws. Since the court upheld laws that make it illegal for domestic violence offenders to possess a firearm, it protected gun control legislation.

However, the court also stated that the Second Amendment protects individuals' rights to possess firearms, lending support to the individual rights interpretation of the Second Amendment. In 2001, after considering Emerson's case, the Fifth Circuit Court of Appeals stated:

> We reject the collective rights and sophisticated collective rights models for interpreting the Second Amendment. We hold . . . that it protects the right of individuals, including those not then actually a member of any militia or engaged in active military service or training, to privately possess and bear their own firearms . . . that are suitable as personal, individual weapons. [13]

Years of contradictory court rulings continue to fuel the gun control debate. Here, Second Amendment supporters rally for their position.

Because the court ruled that the federal laws disarming Emerson were not unconstitutional, gun control proponents claim this ruling as a victory. Because the court stated that it did not support the collective rights interpretation of the Second Amendment, gun rights proponents also claim this ruling as a victory. Rather than clarify the Second Amendment's meaning, court cases such as this have only muddied the debate.

Repeal the Second Amendment

With all the controversy and confusion surrounding the interpretation of the Second Amendment, some Americans believe the simplest way to deal with the amendment is to get rid of it. "The truth about the Second Amendment is something that liberals cannot bear to admit," writes Daniel Lazare, author of *The Frozen Republic: How the Constitution Is Paralyzing Democracy,* in *Harper's* magazine. "The right wing is right. The amendment does confer an individual right to bear arms, and its very presence makes effective gun control in this country all but impossible."[14]

Lazare supports repealing the Second Amendment because without it, there could be no argument about whether gun control does or does not violate the Constitution. Most Americans who favor gun control laws but also believe that the Second Amendment does confer the right of individuals to bear arms, support Lazare's call to repeal the Second Amendment.

Many Americans are frustrated with the stalemate in the Second Amendment debate. Although the call to repeal is not widespread, it reflects the fact that Americans are looking for alternative ways to deal with the Second Amendment because of the polarizing effect of its varied interpretations in the gun control debate.

3

Different Approaches to Gun Control

THERE ARE SEVERAL different approaches to gun control advocated by Americans, which range from requiring background checks of gun purchasers to mandatory registration of all guns by their owners. All of these approaches are aimed at the same result—reducing gun violence in America.

The most common method of gun control is background checks. Background checks are investigations of a gun purchaser's criminal history. Gun dealers conduct these checks to determine if a person is prohibited by law from owning a gun. If a gun purchaser is found to be in a prohibited category, such as being a convicted felon, then the gun dealer does not allow the customer to buy a gun.

Brady law and background checks

Background checks have been required in all states by the Brady law since 1994. This law requires that all federally licensed dealers conduct background checks on gun purchasers. Federally licensed dealers are those who sell guns as a part of their business and have obtained a mandatory federal firearm license (FFL) from the government.

After the Brady law initially was enacted, federally licensed gun dealers contacted the state police in order to check a buyer's background. This could take up to five days. In 1998, the Federal Bureau of Investigation's (FBI) National Instant Criminal Background Check System (NICS) came into use. This national electronic database of criminal records

The Brady law requires federally licensed gun dealers like this Pennsylvania man to perform background checks on all customers.

significantly decreased the time needed to check a gun purchaser's background. A gun dealer can now call NICS and conduct a background check in less than a day.

Brady law results

According to the Bureau of Justice Statistics, the Brady law stopped 840,000 prohibited people from purchasing firearms from March 1994 to the end of 2001. The Bureau of Justice Statistics additionally reports that in 2001, 58 percent of the Brady law rejections were because the purchasers had felony convictions. The other prohibited purchasers were rejected because they were fugitives, they had been convicted of domestic violence, or they had a history of mental illness or drug addiction.

In 2001, the Bureau of Justice issued another report, *Firearm Use by Offenders,* which discusses how firearm use in crime may have been affected by the Brady law. This report discusses the results from surveys of eighteen thousand prison inmates about firearm use in their crimes. The report states that between 1991 and 1997, during which time the Brady law went into effect, the percent of state inmates who purchased a gun from a retail outlet fell from 21 percent to 14 percent.

Brady law advocates claim that these statistics and reports demonstrate the success of the Brady law. They contend that because of the Brady law, fewer criminals are able to get firearms and therefore cannot commit violent crimes. Supporters also cite the fact that since the Brady law has been in effect, violent crime, in particular firearm deaths, has been significantly reduced.

Brady law proponents point to specific incidents to illustrate how the Brady law has stopped felons from committing other crimes. "On April 2, 2000, an individual was prevented from buying a gun in Texas because the NICS check revealed that the buyer had previously been convicted of a felony in

Source: Bureau of Justice Statistics, *Firearm Use by Offenders,* 2002.

Where Criminals Get Guns
Percent of State Inmates Possessing a Firearm

Source of gun	1997	1991
Purchased from		
Retail store:	8.3	14.7
Pawn shop:	3.8	4.2
Flea market:	1.0	1.3
Gun show:	0.7	0.6
Total:	13.9	20.0
Friend or family:	39.6	33.8
Street/illegal source:	39.2	40.8

New Jersey and was still on probation," states the Brady Campaign to Prevent Gun Violence website. "After the individual had been arrested, he stated that it was his intention to use the gun to kill his father in Texas and his mother and stepmother in New Jersey." [15]

Brady law opposition

Although the number of criminals who have obtained guns from retail stores has dropped since the Brady law was enacted, this does not necessarily mean that criminals have not been able to obtain firearms. The *Firearm Use by Offenders* report revealed that up to 80 percent of convicted felons obtained their gun from an illegal source, or friends and family.

Gun control opponents use these statistics to support their claim that the Brady law has not been a factor in America's recent reduction of violent crime. Critics of the Brady law charge that the majority of the purchasers who were stopped from legally obtaining guns because of the Brady law, likely obtained guns illegally.

The gun show loophole

Currently, the Brady law only applies to federally licensed dealers and does not require unlicensed dealers to conduct background checks. Unlicensed gun dealers are people who do not sell guns as part of a business, but occasionally sell firearms from their personal collection of guns. Unlicensed dealers may sell their firearms through ads in the paper, to friends, or at gun shows. At gun shows, both unlicensed and licensed dealers can sell firearms. Currently, eighteen states have state laws that require that all dealers at gun shows conduct background checks.

The ability to purchase a gun at a gun show without undergoing a background check has been termed the "gun show loophole." Supporters of gun control want all states to close the gun show loophole in order to keep criminals, juveniles, and other prohibited purchasers from buying guns from vendors who do not conduct background checks.

A January 2003 editorial in Norfolk, Virginia's the *Virginian-Pilot* illustrated what could happen if states do not close the loophole. "Nothing prevents a criminal who is turned down at the table of a licensed dealer from stepping across the aisle where the wares of an unlicensed dealer are for sale," the editorial states. "All the good that's done by an instant background check at one table is instantly undone by an instant OK to the same criminal at the next one."[16]

Gun control opponents disagree that the gun show loophole is a problem. They claim that making private gun show vendors conduct background checks would prevent only a fraction of criminals from obtaining guns. The *Firearm Use by Offenders* report states than only 1 percent of the surveyed inmates obtained their guns from a gun show. For this reason, critics believe that closing the loophole is a waste of time and money, and would produce limited results.

Waiting periods

Another form of gun control is mandatory waiting periods. A waiting period is the time that gun purchasers must wait between applying to purchase a gun and obtaining the gun. Initially, the Brady law required that all gun purchasers wait five days before obtaining their guns while gun dealers conducted background checks. When the NICS was put into place, the waiting period disappeared because NICS provides most background check results within hours.

Although the Brady law no longer requires a waiting period, eighteen states currently have state laws requiring waiting periods. The reason for these laws is that a waiting period may keep a person from purchasing a gun while in an irrational state. A waiting period is supposed to allow a person to "cool off" in case the person is buying a gun in anger. The theory is that the cooling-off period will prevent crimes of passion by giving the purchaser time to think rationally.

Opponents of waiting periods argue that they do not save lives. Irrational people who intend to kill another person, they claim, will find another weapon to do so if they cannot immediately obtain a gun. Additionally, critics contend that waiting periods actually increase law-abiding citizens' vulnerability to criminals. For example, if a violent estranged husband suddenly threatens his wife, she may feel the need to get a gun

to protect herself. With a waiting period, she would not be able to do so immediately.

In his book *Guns, Crime, and Freedom,* NRA executive vice president Wayne LaPierre illustrates how waiting periods make citizens vulnerable. "In 1990 mass murderer Danny Rolling mutilated five college students in Gainesville, Florida," LaPierre writes. "Fear gripped the college town—there were no suspects. But because that county had a waiting period, the sheriff's department advised residents to go to neighboring counties that had no waiting periods, to buy guns for protection."[17] LaPierre believes that citizens must be able to obtain guns immediately if they have a need to protect themselves.

Banning certain guns

Banning guns is another gun control method advocated as a way to reduce violent crime. Firearms that have been banned or severely restricted in the United States are guns that have been notorious for use in violent crimes and do not have an apparent hunting or self-defense purpose. Banning these weapons potentially reduces criminals' ability to access and use such weapons in crimes.

Assault weapons are an example of the types of guns restricted in the United States. Assault weapons are selective-fire firearms that are capable of fully automatic, semiautomatic, or burst fire. Federal laws enacted in the twentieth century have limited Americans' access to these weapons.

The first federal law to limit assault weapons was aimed at automatic guns. These types of guns automatically feed ammunition into the firearm's chamber and spray multiple bullets when the trigger is pulled. Automatic guns were often used by gangsters in the 1930s. After several Americans called for a law that restricted access to these guns, the federal government passed the National Firearms Act (NFA) in 1934. The NFA restricts the sale of fully automatic weapons.

The Violent Crime Control and Law Enforcement Act, signed into law by President Bill Clinton in 1994, further

A Florida man practices shooting a semiautomatic assault rifle, one of several types of weapons whose use is restricted in the United States.

strengthens the limitation of assault weapons by targeting semiautomatic firearms. This law prohibits the purchase and sale of semiautomatic assault weapons manufactured after September 13, 1994. Semiautomatic assault weapons are guns that fire a single bullet with a pull of the trigger, but automatically load the next bullet into the chamber, allowing for a rapid fire of bullets.

The 1994 federal law prohibits the manufacture of semiautomatic rifles, pistols, and shotguns that accept a detachable magazine and have two or more assault weapon features, such as folding/telescoping stocks. President Clinton signed the Violent Crime Control and Law Enforcement Act into law because he claimed that semiautomatic assault weapons were used by drug traffickers, violent youth gangs, and deranged individuals, and had no legitimate purpose in American society outside of the military.

Reactions to the ban

Proponents of the 1994 ban contend that tragedies such as the Stockton, California, massacre may have been averted if an assault weapons ban had been in place at that time. The Stockton shooting occurred in 1989 at an elementary school, where Patrick Purdy killed five small children and wounded twenty-nine others using a semiautomatic version of the AK-47 assault rifle.

Critics of the 1994 semiautomatic weapons ban claim that the ban does little to reduce gun violence. Reports show that in many states assault weapons were rarely used in firearm homicides even before the ban went into effect. For example, prior to the ban, only 2.5 percent of firearm homicides in Florida involved semiautomatic weapons, none of the thirty-six hundred homicides in Washington, D.C., between 1985 and 1994 involved any kind of rifle, and in Massachusetts only 0.5 percent of homicides from 1986 to 1991 involved assault rifles.

The Violent Crime Control and Law Enforcement Act is set to expire on September 13, 2004. To remain a law, Congress must renew the ban and the president must sign it. The NRA and other ban critics are lobbying Congress in attempt to persuade them not to renew the law.

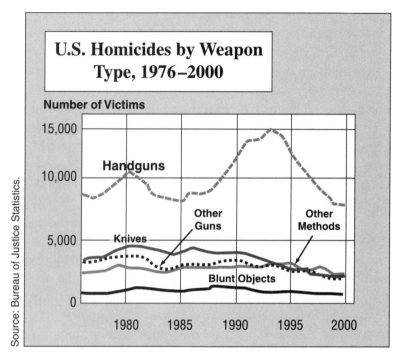

U.S. Homicides by Weapon Type, 1976–2000

Number of Victims

Source: Bureau of Justice Statistics.

Banning handguns

In addition to the federal government banning assault weapons, some cities and districts have enacted laws to ban handguns in their areas, such as Washington, D.C., and Morton Grove, Illinois. The purpose of these bans is to reduce the number of firearm homicides, the majority of which involve handguns. The theory is that by making handguns illegal, less will circulate and be available for use in crimes.

Although many mainstream gun control organizations are proponents of banning "Saturday night specials," which are cheap, easily concealable handguns that are poorly made, most of these organizations do not favor an outright ban of all handguns. However, there are certain organizations, such as the Washington, D.C.–based Violence Policy Center, and individuals who believe a national handgun ban is necessary to reduce gun violence. Josh Sugarmann, author of *Every Handgun Is Aimed at You*, writes:

> The call to ban handguns is not inspired by a hatred of guns. It is a response to the very real blood price that our nation has paid for the explosive growth of our handgun population over the past

generation. More than two out of three of the one million Americans who have died by firearms violence since 1962 were killed with handguns—a tally now in excess of 670,000. [18]

Gun rights groups argue that handgun bans do not reduce gun violence. They claim that in towns and cities where handguns have been banned, there has been little to no reduction of violent crime. Former executive director of the NRA Institute for Legislative Action, James Jay Baker, argued against bans and strict gun legislation at the 2000 NRA convention, citing Washington, D.C., as an example of how handgun bans do not work.

Despite the fact that Washington, D.C., has some of the toughest firearm laws in the United States, including a ban on handguns registered after 1977, Baker said that the district is filled with violent incidents. At the NRA convention, he discussed the shooting of seven students at the National Zoo in Washington, D.C., in 2000 by sixteen-year-old Antoine Jones. "If disarming Americans were a solution to anything, our nation's capital would be crime-free, a gun-controller's paradise," Baker said. "But instead, our nation's capital remains plagued by criminals like Antoine Jones, who pulled the trigger that sunny day at the zoo." [19]

Tracking gun ownership

Tracking is an approach to gun control where, if instituted, the U.S. government would maintain records of all the legal firearms and gun owners throughout the country. The purpose of tracking is to make it easier for law enforcement to find and convict criminals who have committed gun crimes. Gun registration is one proposed way to track America's gun owners.

Gun registration would entail government recording all legal gun sales, including the names of the sellers and owners involved in the sales, in a database. If registration were required by federal law, every time a gun were sold, the gun seller and purchaser would have to submit information regarding the sale to the government. The government would then have detailed records of who owns what firearms throughout the country.

With a national gun registry in place, if police officers discovered a gun at a crime scene, they would be able to use the registry to locate the gun's last legal owner. This could help law enforcement find out who used the gun in the crime and ultimately result in a quicker capture of the criminal.

Fighting crime or confiscation?

Aside from helping police solve crimes, another reason for mandatory registration is that it could potentially reduce crime. With a registry in place, those considering committing a crime with a gun would likely think twice if they knew that the police could easily track the gun back to them.

Gun control opponents vehemently oppose registration. They claim that a gun registry could allow the government to confiscate guns from legal gun owners at some point in the future. They point to the consequences that New York gun owners faced after a mandatory gun registry of rifle and shotgun owners was enacted.

In 1967, New York City passed an ordinance requiring citizens to register and obtain a permit to own a rifle or a shotgun. In 1991, the city banned the private possession of certain semiautomatic rifles and shotguns. The New York City Police Department notified the New Yorkers who had registered prior to the ban that any of the firearms covered by the ban had to be surrendered, rendered inoperable, or removed from the city. Those notified were directed to send back a sworn statement that showed what they had done with those firearms. Gun rights advocates claim that this is what would likely happen to all U.S. gun owners if a national registration were required.

Ballistic fingerprinting

Another controversial tracking method is ballistic fingerprinting. Each gun leaves a unique marking, called a ballistic fingerprint, on a bullet when it is shot from the gun. If ballistic fingerprinting were mandated nationwide, gun manufacturers would have to submit to the government ballistic fingerprints of every firearm their companies produced. The government would maintain records of the ballistic fingerprints and the guns from which they were shot.

Like registration, the purpose of ballistic fingerprinting is to help the police solve gun crimes more rapidly. If a national

Maryland police search for the Washington, D.C., sniper. Some believe the case may have easily been solved with a national ballistic fingerprinting database.

ballistic fingerprint database were in place and a bullet were found at a crime scene, the police could compare the marking left on the bullet to the ballistic fingerprints in the database. If the ballistic fingerprint matched one in the database, police officers would then know what gun had left the mark on the bullet. At that point, law enforcement could start tracing the gun to its owner.

Effective or expensive?

The 2002 Washington, D.C., sniper shootings is often cited as an example of a case that could have been solved more easily with a ballistic fingerprint database. During the sniper shootings, law enforcement officials were able to compare the ballistic fingerprints found on each of the bullets at the individual shootings. Based on these comparisons, they were able to determine that the sniper victims were all shot by the same gun.

However, without a national ballistic fingerprinting database, until the snipers were apprehended, law enforcement agencies could not determine which gun was used in the shootings. If law enforcement had been able to determine which rifle was used early on in the investigation, supporters of ballistic fingerprinting contend that law enforcement would have been able to trace the rifle to its last legal owner. This could have led them to the snipers more quickly.

At the end of 2002, Maryland and New York were the only two states with state ballistic fingerprinting databases in place. Although advocates claim that in time these states will benefit by being able to quickly solve gun crimes, critics claim that the state ballistic systems are expensive and ineffective.

According to John R. Lott Jr., author of *More Guns, Less Crime,* it cost Maryland $1.1 million to start its program, and $750,000 every year to maintain. In 2001, New York's system cost $4.5 million to launch and its annual maintenance cost was not publicized. In 2002, Lott wrote in the *National Review,* "And what was the specific benefit? Almost zero. The programs have not helped solve a single violent crime in either state; they have so far been used only to identify two handguns stolen from a Maryland gun shop."[20]

Licensing guns

Another gun control approach is the mandatory licensing of gun owners. If a national gun-licensing mandate were in place, all gun owners would be required to obtain licenses before they could purchase firearms. In order to obtain a gun license, a person would have to fulfill strict requirements such as completing a more thorough background check than currently required by the Brady law and passing a firearm safety exam.

The purpose of gun licensing is to ensure that gun owners are properly trained so that they are less likely to misuse or unsafely store their firearms. Advocates of gun licensing claim that in addition to reducing gun misuse, licensing would keep guns out of the hands of criminals because of the proposed, more intense background checks.

David Hemenway of the Harvard School of Public Health writes in a 1998 edition of the *New England Journal of Medicine:*

> The United States has more cars per capita than any other developed nation. Because of reasonable policies to regulate automobiles and roadways, we now have one of the lowest motor vehicle fatality rates. We are also a society with more guns per capita than any other developed nation. We can remain a nation with many guns yet control our gun-injury problem if we take reasonable steps to make firearms safer and to keep them out of the wrong hands. [21]

Critics of licensing charge that it would not reduce crime because those who plan to use guns in crimes would not obtain licenses and instead would illegally acquire their guns. Licensing, like every gun control approach, provokes intense debate because compelling reasons can be found to both support and oppose it. Because reports, statistics, and surveys that both support and oppose each gun control approach can be found, it is not yet possible to definitively determine if any approach achieves its goal of reducing gun violence.

4

Guns and Kids

ON THE MORNING of February 29, 2000, six-year-old Kayla Rolland was attending Theo J. Buell Elementary School in Mount Morris Township, Michigan. As she was walking up the stairs from one class to another, a six-year-old class-mate called out to her. He told Kayla that he did not like her. Kayla turned around and said, "So?" In response, the boy shot her with a Davis .32 semiautomatic handgun. The bullet struck Kayla in the right shoulder and tore through her vital organs. Paramedics were called but they were unable to help. Kayla was then rushed to Hurley Medical Center, where she was pronounced dead.

Authorities investigating the shooting learned that the boy lived with his uncle and discovered that the house where they lived was a meeting place for people who traded guns for drugs. The boy apparently had found a loaded handgun under a pile of blankets in the house and brought it to school.

After the news about where the boy found the gun was pub-licized, there was heated public debate about whether or not the shooting was the result of the boy's violent upbringing or his access to firearms, or a combination of these and other fac-tors. During the same time period, several other high-profile tragedies involving guns and children stunned the nation. This prompted Americans to discuss not only the cause of, but also how to solve, the youth gun violence problem.

More than murder

Gun violence takes the lives of nearly nine children each day. Homicides such as school shootings are just part of the problem. Another factor in firearm fatalities among youth are accidental shootings. Accidental shootings occur when a child obtains a parent's or other adult's firearm, usually without the adult's permission, and the gun goes off when the child plays with it.

A recent example of an accidental shooting occurred in Houston, Texas. On January 27, 2003, seven-year-old Dovie Caroline Hill, daughter of Glen Hill, a Houston police officer, died after she shot herself in the head with a pistol. She found the loaded gun unattended in her parents' bedroom. Police later found two loaded revolvers and an unloaded rifle in the bedroom. The guns were not locked or hidden away.

In addition to accidental shootings, suicide also significantly contributes to firearm fatalities among young people. From 1980 to 1997, the rate of suicide among persons aged

Gun violence kills almost nine children every day. Child gun violence remains a central issue in the gun control debate.

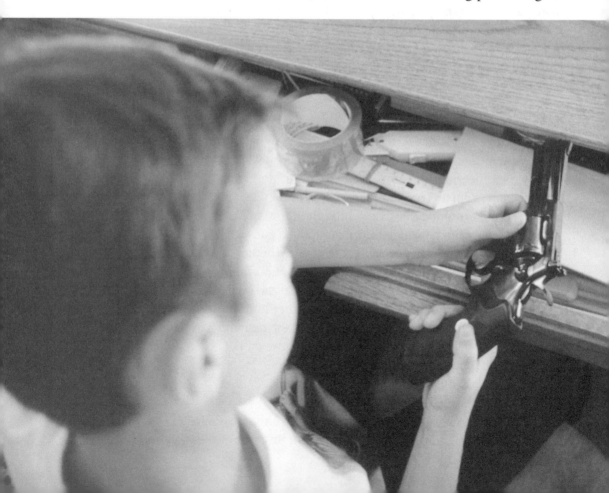

fifteen to nineteen years old increased by 11 percent. According to the Centers for Disease Control and Prevention, 60 percent of this increase was due to suicides with guns.

Escalating debates

Whether due to homicides, accidental shootings, or suicides, tragedies involving children and guns have shocked the American public. As a result, youth gun violence has become a hot topic in politics. Often following high-profile shootings of children, government leaders debate what causes youth gun tragedies and how to prevent such tragedies in the future.

For example, within twenty-four hours of the 1998 school shooting in Jonesboro, Arkansas, gun control and gun violence were being discussed in Congress. In 1998, at Westside Middle School in Jonesboro, two male students aged eleven and thirteen set off a fire alarm to lure the students outside. As the students assembled outside, the two boys, both wearing camouflage, lay down in the woods nearby. The boys opened fire on the unsuspecting students, killing five people.

Some Americans believed that the Jonesboro shooting was due to the boys' easy access to firearms. The day following the shooting, congressional member Charles Schumer agreed that the Jonesboro boys' access to the guns was partially responsible for the shooting and proposed that guns should be required to have childproof safety locks.

Potential causes

Other government leaders and Americans disagreed with Representative Schumer. For example, the NRA spokespeople expressed their horror at the Jonesboro tragedy, but also stated their organization's opinion that the shooting was the result of a morality problem among children, and not easy access to firearms.

Representative Schumer's proposal was defeated, but discussions about the cause of youth gun violence have continued. Some Americans agree that easy access to guns is a factor in youth gun violence. Others uphold the NRA's theory that youth gun violence is due to morality problems among children. Still other Americans attribute the youth gun violence

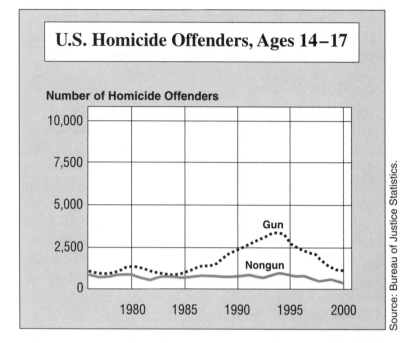

U.S. Homicide Offenders, Ages 14–17

Number of Homicide Offenders

Gun

Nongun

Source: Bureau of Justice Statistics.

problem to causes such as the lack of gun safety training among children, an increase in gang violence, and the influence of violent videos, toys, and games on today's youth.

No matter what the cause of firearm fatalities among youth, the fact is that thousands of children continue to die each year from gunshot wounds. According to the National Center for Injury Prevention and Control, in the year 2000, 1,007 Americans aged nineteen and under committed suicide using firearms; 193 youth died due to accidental shootings; and 1,776 died because of firearm homicides.

CAP laws

Although Americans disagree about the causes of youth violence, they do agree that the number of children who die each year due to gun violence is unacceptable. As a result, several different ways to decrease youth firearm fatalities have been proposed. Enacting Child Access Prevention (CAP) laws is one way to potentially reduce youth gun deaths, and it is specifically targeted at reducing accidental shootings.

CAP laws, also known as safe storage laws, punish adults who do not take reasonable efforts to keep their guns inaccessible to children. CAP laws require that adults either store loaded guns in places that children cannot easily get to or lock their firearms so only adults can access them. The purpose of such laws is to force adults to carefully store their firearms so children cannot obtain and use them.

Florida became the first state to pass a CAP law in 1989. By 2002, nineteen states had CAP laws. In a state with a CAP law, if a child obtains an improperly stored and loaded gun in an adult's house, the adult is criminally liable and can be severely penalized. For example, in Florida, if a minor obtains an adult's gun and uses it to harm himself or someone else, the adult is charged with a felony.

Do CAP laws work?

CAP law proponents claim that state CAP laws have resulted in significant reductions of unintentional shooting deaths. In Florida, for example, unintentional shooting deaths dropped

After losing a friend to gun violence, this Indiana teenager pleads with a Senate committee to enact Child Access Prevention laws in his state.

more than 50 percent the first year after a CAP law was passed. Additionally, CAP law advocates use examples, such as the death of Dovie Hill, to demonstrate why CAP laws are needed.

Law enforcement officers like Dovie Hill's father receive significant training on how to handle and store guns. With this training, these adults should have a good understanding of how to safely store their weapons and prevent their children from obtaining them. But, according to CAP law proponents, Dovie Hill's father's negligence shows that even training cannot stop accidents. The guns in Dovie Hill's house were left loaded and unattended.

"Really, the lesson here is, civilian or police officer, guns need to be secured," said Hans Marticiuc, president of the Houston Police Officer Union, commenting on Dovie's death. "Do whatever you need to try to keep these things out of children's hands." [22] CAP law proponents claim that safe storage legislation forces adults to be more responsible because of the threat of criminal charges if they are not.

Opponents of CAP laws charge that such laws violate a person's ability to defend himself. Critics claim that CAP laws can impede an adult's ability to get to the gun in an emergency such as a burglary. Additionally, they contend that determining what is safe gun storage should be the gun owner's, not the government's, responsibility.

Loaded indicators

Another method aimed at reducing youth gun accidents is to require firearm manufacturers to install loaded chamber indicators on the handguns they produce. A loaded chamber indicator is a small device found on some pistols that displays a warning when the chamber contains a cartridge. Currently, firearm manufacturers are not required by law to place loaded chamber indicators on their handguns.

On handguns with loaded chamber indicators, usually the indicator is a pin built into the mechanism of the pistol. If a cartridge is in the chamber, and the action is closed, the pin protrudes from the gun, showing that it is loaded. The theory behind this preventative mechanism is that if a person, including a child, could immediately see that a gun were loaded, then the person would be more careful when handling the gun.

Proponents of mandating loaded chamber indicators claim that indicators would reduce youth accidental shootings. Children could be taught not to touch any gun with an indicator that signaled the gun was loaded. Additionally, indicators could help parents who own guns store their guns more safely. Gun owners would immediately know by their guns' indicators if their guns were unloaded or loaded. This could reduce the chance that adults would leave a loaded gun unattended in the house.

However, mandatory indicators could result in more accidents. People could come to rely on indicators to let them know whether or not a gun were "safe." If an indicator on a gun failed, people may still treat the gun as though it were unloaded, because they had learned to rely on indicators to let them know how to treat a gun. This could result in an accidental shooting. Critics of mandating indicators instead recommend that people should be taught to treat all firearms as though they were loaded. They contend that this is a more foolproof way of preventing accidental shootings.

Teaching gun safety

Gun safety training for young children teaches them what to do if they find an unattended gun, whether it is loaded or not. Firearm safety training includes teaching children that if they find a gun, to not touch it and to find an adult. The purpose of this training is to prevent children from playing with a gun that they might find.

A popular gun safety program is the NRA's Eddie Eagle Gun Safe Program, which was launched in 1988. The Eddie Eagle program is led by a character, Eddie Eagle, and is targeted to elementary school aged children. Eddie Eagle teaches children to "Stop, Don't Touch, Leave the Area, Tell an Adult" when they find a gun. This program is on video and is also presented live across the United States. According to the NRA website, the Eddie Eagle program had reached over 16 million children by 2003.

The NRA's Eddie Eagle is the mascot for one of many training programs aimed at teaching gun safety to young children.

Since Eddie Eagle began, National Health Statistics reports a 56 percent drop in fatal firearm injuries. Critics argue that this drop has been due to tougher gun laws, not the Eddie Eagle program. However, the program has received several awards, including the silver Award of Merit from the Youth Activities Division of the National Safety Council and a Citation for Outstanding Community Service from the National Safety Council.

After studying the Eddie Eagle program and its results, some schools around the country decided to provide mandatory gun safety programs as part of their students' curriculum. In 2001, Carroll County Schools in Maryland became the nation's first school district to require that gun safety be taught as a part of health and life classes from kindergarten through twelfth grade. The program is modeled after the Eddie Eagle program and was developed by school officials, parents, teachers, and law enforcement representatives.

Youth gun programs

In addition to gun safety programs for young children, there are also firearm safety programs in place for older children and teenagers. These supervised programs involve training older children how to use guns, as opposed to teaching them to stay away from guns. Gun safety training for older children consists of certified instructors teaching them how to safely handle, shoot, and store firearms.

One of the purposes of gun training programs for older children is to familiarize the children with guns so that they will not be tempted to seek out guns on their own and use them without supervision. These programs are also meant to teach children self-discipline and control.

The Boy Scouts of America and the 4-H Club support the belief that sport shooting instills good character, and each provides various shooting instruction and contests for their members. According to the 4-H Shooting Sports website:

> 4-H uses shooting sports to teach youth development. Our programs are valuable for helping young people develop self-confidence, personal discipline, responsibility, teamwork, self-esteem and sportsmanship. The discipline and self-control required for responsible firearms use carries over into many other aspects of life. [23]

Solving it themselves

Learning how to treat firearms safely is not the only way young people have become involved in the fight against gun violence. Some youth have joined anti–gun violence organizations in an attempt to help reduce gun fatalities. Working with these organizations, young people fight gun violence by lobbying the government for stricter gun laws, educating other youth about the effects of gun violence, and promoting nonviolent activities for children.

The Ymedia campaign in Hampton Roads, Virginia, is an example of a youth-led program fighting gun violence. The national Ymedia program provides guidance and support to youth, aged eight to eighteen, who are interested in working together to develop media campaigns centered on the issues of young people. Members of Ymedia develop and submit their media campaign ideas to the national Ymedia program and then are provided with guidance on how to run their campaigns.

The Hampton Roads Ymedia campaign's purpose is to educate young people about the devastating effects of gun violence and about ways kids can avoid getting involved with guns. Ymedia members from five high schools in the Hampton Roads area have used a variety of methods to illustrate the severity of gun violence. For example, one member organized a "Silent March" of shoes to represent the number of Virginia youngsters who have been killed by guns.

Other Hampton Roads Ymedia members have spoken at city council meetings about what the city can do to reduce gun violence among its youth. For example, they spoke about the need for more recreational centers and city-provided youth

Some youth organizations have staged silent shoe marches like this one to demonstrate the devastating effects of gun violence.

activities. Ymedia members explained that if the city governments provided more fun, youth-oriented activities then kids
would be less likely to get involved with violence and guns.

Co/Motion

Co/Motion is another organization that gets young people
involved in a national campaign to end gun violence.
Co/Motion provides training on how to run projects and gives
grants of money to youth-developed programs that deal with
issues young people face, including gun control. Co/Motion
publicizes these programs in its quarterly newsletter and on
its website.

Youth can also get involved in Co/Motion through its annual "Drawing the Line on Gun Violence" poster contest, which
Co/Motion first sponsored in February 2002. That year, high
school students across the country were invited to submit
posters depicting the impact of gun violence. After receiving
one thousand submissions, thirteen winners were selected and
were honored in Washington, D.C. Select posters designed by
the winners appeared on billboards across the country. Theo
Milonopoulos, a ninth grader from Los Angeles, won the grand
prize for his poster "Guns Kill America's Future."

Student pledge against gun violence

In other efforts to solve the youth gun problem, students
across the United States have pledged to avoid using guns to
settle disputes. The Student Pledge Against Gun Violence is
a nationwide pledge that students sign on October 8, the annual Day of National Concern About Young People and Gun
Violence.

By signing this pledge, students agree to never carry a gun
to school, to never resolve a personal problem or dispute with
a gun, and to use their influence to keep friends from resolv-
ing disputes with guns. On October 8, 1998, over 1 million
students signed the pledge. This number rose to over 3 million in 2002.

Students take the pledge seriously even though no one but
themselves would know if they broke the pledge. Saiida
Hodges, a senior at Murray Bergtraum High School in

Manhattan, explained why she takes the pledge seriously, "If you break it . . . you feel punishment in your heart."[24]

Cool-No-Violence Peace Project

In addition to fighting gun violence through organized programs, teenagers have individually tackled the gun violence problem. Danielle Shimotakahara, age fifteen, of Coos County, Oregon, developed the Cool-No-Violence Peace Project. This project's goal is to stop young kids from playing violent video games that involve shooting.

Shimotakahara believes that these games contribute toward kids becoming violent in real life. She got the idea for her project after she learned that the two teenaged gunmen at Columbine High School were avid players of a violent video game. Shimotakahara then noted the kinds of video games students she knew played.

She watched her peers play one video game where an animated person points a gun at people. By using the controls, the player can have the animated person pull the gun's trigger. Blood splatters after the person shoots someone in the game. "My pastor . . . told me that games are supposed to prepare kids for real life situations," Shimotakahara said. "So what does a game that rips bodies to pieces and explodes body parts and splatters blood on the screen teach kids to prepare for in real life?"[25]

After watching her friends play violent games, Shimotakahara decided to do something. She persuaded eight local businesses, including restaurants, to remove violent video games from their premises. Additionally, she played a role in getting the Coos Bay City Council and Oregon state legislature to pass a resolution requiring businesses to label violent video games in order to restrict children's access to them.

The surgeon general report

With so many approaches to reducing youth gun violence, it is difficult to know what ways are the most effective. In an attempt to determine this, the U.S. Department of Health and Human Services analyzed youth violence and the programs addressing it. In 2001, it issued its results in *Youth Violence,*

A Report of the Surgeon General. In this report, the U.S. Department of Health and Human Services suggests that skill building and parent training programs are among the best ways to reduce violence.

Some believe that the extreme violence of video games contributes toward gun violence among children.

Skill building programs teach self-control and interpersonal problem-solving skills to children so that they have other ways of dealing with conflict than violence. Parent training programs are where parents of at-risk-for-violence children are taught how to monitor their children's behavior, provide effective discipline, and reinforce nonviolent behavior. The purpose of these programs is to intervene early on in the lives of children who are at risk of being involved in violence. The programs' goals are to instill in the children the belief that there are other options to solving problems than violence and to teach them what these options are.

Decreasing violence

In its report, the U.S. Department of Health and Human Services also listed other factors that are linked to decreasing firearm violence. After studying the significant decrease of firearm fatalities among youth aged nineteen and under from 1993 to 1998—when 5,751 youth firearm fatalities dropped to 3,792—the U.S. Department of Health and Human Services determined possible reasons for the reduction.

The *Youth Violence, A Report of the Surgeon General* concludes that causes of the decrease in firearm use among youth were likely due to a decline in youth involvement in the crack market, crackdowns on gun carrying and illegal gun purchases, longer sentences for crimes involving guns, a strong economy, and more crime and violence prevention programs. It is probable that not one, but many of these factors had to do with youth gun violence diminishing.

5

Can Gun Violence Be Reduced Without Gun Control?

BECAUSE OF THE controversy over whether or not gun control is effective at reducing gun violence, many Americans have sought alternative solutions to the gun violence problem. Rather than implement new gun control laws, approaches ranging from manufacturers producing "safe" guns to the government more strictly enforcing current gun laws have been proposed as ways to reduce gun violence.

One of the more controversial alternatives to gun control is to require gun owners to use and manufacturers to produce "safe" guns. A safe gun is a firearm that features a safety mechanism that makes it difficult for any person, except the gun's owner, to fire it. This reduces the chance of a criminal obtaining a gun during a burglary or using a gun against its owner. Additionally, these guns are designed to reduce accidental shootings among children because even if a child gets a hold of a safe gun, it is designed so that the child cannot shoot it.

Trigger locks

One way to make a gun "safe" is to install a trigger lock on it. In order to fire a gun with a trigger lock, the gun owner must first unlock it with a key or combination that only the gun owner will have. Although both gun control proponents and opponents support the use of trigger locks, they disagree on mandating their use. Gun control proponents believe that

manufacturers should be required to install trigger locks on all guns, while gun rights advocates believe that the use of a trigger lock should be a choice left to the gun owner.

In 2003, Maryland enacted a law requiring that all new guns sold in the state have integrated trigger locks installed. Although the trigger lock law does not place restrictions on who can obtain guns, and how they can obtain them, opponents of the law claim that it is a form of gun control. Specifically, critics charge that the Maryland law is gun banning in disguise. They point to the fact that in 2003, there were only six models of handguns and locks on the market that met Maryland's requirements.

"I believe it's a restraint of trade," Carl Roy, owner of Maryland Small Arms, an indoor shooting range and weapons distributor, stated. "It's basically going to ban new guns in the state. We've already had a number of distributors saying they won't ship guns into the state." [26] According to Roy and other gun shop owners, manufacturers will cut back their distribution to Maryland, putting several dealers out of business.

Despite the opposition, State Senator Brian Frosh, who supports the Maryland trigger lock measure, argued, "How do you balance saving the life of a child against the prospect that sales might decrease somewhat? To me, when you look at the balance, it comes out heavily on the side of saving lives."[27]

Smart guns

Many who agree with Senator Frosh's sentiment also advocate the manufacturing of "smart" guns. Smart guns are another form of safe guns. They are firearms that are equipped with technology that ensures recognized users can only fire the guns.

Provided the technology works, if a gun is handled by anyone other than the recognized owner, that person will not be able to fire the weapon. This technology could help reduce the number of criminals who are able to obtain a police officer's gun during a skirmish and use it against the officer, in addition to decreasing the number of children who shoot unattended guns.

The New Jersey Senate approved a bill in 2002 that would require all new guns sold in the state to be smart guns three years after user-identification technology becomes commercially available. As with the trigger locks, the mandated use of smart gun technology, and not the technology itself, is controversial.

Advocates of the New Jersey bill lauded it as a way to reduce firearm accidents. However, New Jersey gun owners argue that if this bill becomes a law, it will effectively end the sale of handguns in the state. They claim that when technology makes smart guns possible, few manufacturers will sell them, and this equates to a ban on handguns. As of 2003, there were no firearms in production that incorporated smart gun technology and the prototypes that have been developed were still being tested.

Suing manufacturers

Suing firearm manufacturers is another method used to reduce gun violence. Manufacturers are sued for not producing "safe" products, resulting in firearm deaths. The goal of many of these lawsuits is to persuade the manufacturers to produce guns with trigger locks. On March 17, 2000, the first settlement agreement was reached between a gun manufacturer, Smith & Wesson, and various cities and counties suing them. Cities such as Detroit and St. Louis filed lawsuits against Smith & Wesson for damages due to gun violence.

Smith & Wesson settled these lawsuits by agreeing to various terms, such as designing every firearm so that a child under the age of six could not operate the guns. They also agreed to devote 2 percent of the company's gross revenues to the development of "smart" guns, which can only be fired by an authorized user, and within two years of the settlement, all Smith & Wesson pistols were to be manufactured with internal trigger locks.

Gun control advocates, including former president Bill Clinton, hailed this settlement as a victory that would result in safer guns and would save lives. However, gun rights organizations blasted the agreement, stating that the judicial process should not be abused to punish companies for violence that people, not companies, caused.

Abuse of the system?

The NRA and other gun rights organizations have persuaded many legislators that suing gun manufacturers is an abuse of the judicial system. "The plaintiffs in these cases," said Lawrence G. Keane, representing the National Shooting Sports Foundation, to Congress in 2003,

> do not allege that members of the firearms industry have broken any of our nation's over 20,000 firearm laws. Instead, they allege that the sale of a legal product in accordance with an extensive regulatory system somehow causes crime and that the industry is subverting the law to funnel firearms to the so-called criminal market. These allegations are both highly offensive and patently false.[28]

In April 2003, the U.S. House of Representatives passed a bill that would protect gun makers and dealers from civil lawsuits involving the misuse of their products. The bill was heading to the Senate for a vote. If it passes the Senate and is signed into law, the kinds of lawsuits Americans can file against

firearms manufacturers and dealers will be limited. With the passage of the bill, mandating trigger locks and other safety features through court verdicts would effectively be stopped.

In response to a collection of lawsuits, Smith & Wesson agreed to implement several safety measures, including the use of trigger locks.

Concealed carry laws

A significantly different, and just as controversial, way to decrease gun violence is to loosen concealed carry weapon (CCW) laws. CCW laws restrict whether or not Americans can carry guns hidden from view. Less restrictive CCW laws would allow more people to carry concealed guns while in public.

The idea behind its approach is to create doubt in the minds of criminals. If people are allowed to carry guns hidden from view, criminals will not know if their intended victims are carrying guns or not. As a result, criminals may be deterred from carrying out their assault or robbery because they are afraid that their intended victims may defend themselves with a gun. Studies correlating less-restrictive CCW laws with a reduction in violent crime provide supporting evidence for this approach.

Because of this evidence, the NRA and other pro–gun rights groups are proponents of carrying concealed guns as a means of reducing gun violence. They have lobbied state legislators to allow citizens to carry concealed weapons. As a result, over thirty states now allow their citizens to carry concealed weapons.

John R. Lott Jr., a criminologist, supports CCW in his book *More Guns, Less Crime,* which he wrote after examining year-ly FBI crime data from 1977 to 1992. Based on his research,

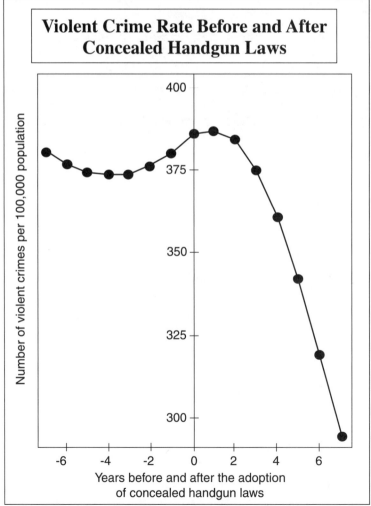

Violent Crime Rate Before and After Concealed Handgun Laws

Source: John R. Lott Jr., *More Guns, Less Crime: Understanding Crime and Gun-Control Laws,* 1998.

Lott concluded that if CCW laws existed in every state in 1992, these laws would have prevented about sixteen hundred murders and forty-eight hundred rapes. According to Lott's study, after concealed weapons were allowed in the studied counties, murders fell by about 8 percent, rapes 5 percent, and aggravated assaults 7 percent.

Critics of CCW laws refute this claim. "While there might have been some superficial statistical evidence that supported Lott when he did his initial work," said Stanford law professor John J. Donahue III, "now that we've got the experience of the '90s behind us, we see that we've gotten those huge drops in crime everywhere—much bigger in states that did not adopt [concealed carry weapon laws]."[29] CCW opponents argue that the drop in crime has been due to tougher gun laws such as the Brady law, the reduction of the crack-cocaine market, and a good economy.

Gun safety courses

A less controversial way to reduce gun violence, supported by many Americans, is to teach adults gun safety. This method is used primarily to reduce accidental shootings among adults. Adult gun safety lessons teach gun owners how to properly handle guns and how to prevent misuse of firearms. Additionally, gun safety training teaches gun owners how to safely store firearms so children will not be able to access their guns.

Gun safety is already a requirement for many gun owners because firearm instruction is part of mandatory hunter education programs. Forty-five states require that either all hunters, or hunters under a certain age, attend hunter education programs. Because of these requirements, hundreds of thousands of Americans learn gun safety each year.

Pennsylvania began conducting formal hunter education courses in 1959. Since 1982, Pennsylvania's hunter-trapper education courses have been mandatory for all first-time hunters. Pennsylvania's gun safety program teaches tips to hunters and others who attend the class. Such tips include not to rely on safety mechanisms when handling a gun because such mechanisms can fail, to unload a firearm when it is not in use, and to never point a loaded or an unloaded gun at something that the gun owner does not want to shoot.

Many in the state claim that this program has helped decrease Pennsylvania's firearm accidents. According to the Pennsylvania Game Commission, more than 1.7 million students have been certified through the training program to date, and statistics show that hunting fatalities and injuries from firearms have declined nearly 80 percent since the program began.

Mandate training?

Although firearm safety for hunters is required in a majority of states, firearm safety classes for gun owners who are not hunters are not typically required. Despite this fact, thousands of Americans voluntarily attend gun safety classes each year. Nationwide, thirty-eight thousand NRA instructors and coaches conduct firearm safety and proficiency programs, reaching more than seven hundred thousand participants annually.

Gun safety is a popular alternative to gun control because both gun control proponents and gun rights advocates agree on the benefits of gun safety training, such as helping to prevent accidental shootings both by adults and children. However, there remains controversy between the two groups concerning whether or not gun safety should be mandatory.

Gun control proponents want gun safety classes to be a mandatory requirement for all gun owners in the United States. Gun rights proponents believe that gun safety instruction should be voluntary because they consider most mandatory requirements of gun owners a violation of the Second Amendment.

Enforce existing laws

In recent years, both sides of the gun control debate have discovered more common ground and have focused their energies on working together. As a result, one of the most popular alternatives to gun control that provokes the least amount of debate is to implement programs that enforce the over twenty thousand gun laws already in place throughout the United States.

In many cities and states, violators of gun laws often receive limited sentences. As a result, these gun laws are not as effective as they could be at reducing gun violence. If the laws were enforced, more violators would be prosecuted and possibly deter others from committing similar crimes. For this reason, city, state, and federal governments have started programs aimed at enforcing existing laws.

A boy participates in a firearm safety seminar. Safety training for gun owners is a popular alternative to gun control.

Project Exile

Project Exile was developed in 1997 by the U.S. attorney general's office in Richmond, Virginia. The program's primary goal is to more strictly enforce gun laws by giving tougher sentences to violators of such laws. The strategy of Project Exile is to target armed criminals arrested by local police for routine crimes and charge them with seldom used federal gun charges, such as obliterating serial numbers on weapons. Federal charges carry strict, mandatory sentences, which are often more severe than state charges. Those convicted are sent to out-of-state federal penitentiaries, which is where the name "exile" comes from. The program is supported by groups as varied as state police, politicians, the NRA, and the Brady Center to Prevent Gun Violence.

A major part of Project Exile is an outreach/education effort to get the message to the criminals about Richmond's program and its crackdown on gun use. A coalition of business, community, and church leaders promoted the project in Richmond, and in 1997 the media carried the message "An illegal gun will get you five years in federal prison" on billboards, radio ads, and buses. After the program began, gun seizures went up and Richmond's homicide rate declined from 139 murders in 1997 to 72 in 1999.

Many officials, including the former attorney general of Texas, have emulated Virginia's Project Exile and have instituted similar programs in their own states.

Project Disarm

Some critics attribute the decline of Richmond's murders to the reduction of the crack trade market across the nation. However, many politicians and organizations believe that Project Exile has been successful in reducing gun crime and consider it an example of gun control and gun rights organizations working together in a positive fashion. As a result, other cities have followed Richmond's example.

In 2002, Cincinnati implemented Project Disarm, based on the Project Exile program. With Project Disarm, the Cincinnati police work with the federal Bureau of Alcohol, Tobacco, Firearms and Explosives (ATF) and county and federal prosecutors so that more local gun violators are prosecuted at the federal level. Before the program began, Cincinatti police confiscated about nine hundred guns per year from gun law violators. In 2002, it was estimated that the number might surpass twelve hundred.

The case of Christopher Godby represents the potential of Project Disarm to remove violent criminals from the streets. Because a previous felony conviction disqualified Godby from buying guns legally, he enlisted other people to buy guns for him. Police said that Godby resold the guns on the street, one of which was used by a teenager to shoot a two year old.

Godby was sentenced to ten years in prison after he pleaded guilty to illegally acquiring eleven guns. If Godby had received punishment through the state system, rather than at the federal level, it is possible he could have plea-bargained and received a sentence as short as eighteen months.

Several other cities such as San Francisco and Philadelphia have implemented programs modeled after Project Disarm and Project Exile. The federal government's leaders have been impressed with the results and have implemented a similar program at the federal level, called Project Safe Neighborhoods.

Project Safe Neighborhoods

When John Ashcroft took over as U.S. attorney general in 2000, he promised that his administration would work harder at prosecuting gun crimes. Ashcroft believes that if the illegal possession of guns in the United States is reduced, then

Try Doing it from a Federal Prison.

In 2003 government officials unveiled an advertising campaign that threatened federal prosecution for gun crimes that was part of Project Safe Neighborhoods.

violent crime will also be reduced. To accomplish his goal, he hired more prosecutors to pursue people who buy guns illegally and he implemented Project Safe Neighborhoods.

Project Safe Neighborhoods is a national program carried out by a partnership between the National District Attorneys Association, the International Chiefs of Police, the National Crime Prevention Council, and the ATF. Like Project Exile, the program diverts gun-related cases from state court to federal court, where penalties are harsher.

Speaking to a conference of federal, state, and local law enforcement officials in Philadelphia, Ashcroft said 10,600 suspected offenders were charged with federal gun violations in 2002, compared to 8,054 who faced federal gun charges in 2000, the year he became attorney general. Project Safe Neighborhoods accounted for 7,747 of the 2002 federal gun charges. Of those charged, 93 percent of the offenders were sentenced to prison, 71 percent of whom received terms of three years or more.

Both gun rights and gun control organizations support Project Safe Neighborhoods. Gun rights advocates support Project Safe Neighborhoods and similar programs because they crack down on criminals, a gun rights approach to reducing gun violence. Gun control organizations approve of such programs because existing gun laws are enforced. Although the gun control debate continues, these programs have proved that it is not impossible for gun rights and gun control organizations to find common ground and work together to reduce gun violence.

Notes

Introduction

1. Quoted in Peter Harry Brown and Daniel G. Abel, *Outgunned: Up Against the NRA*. New York: Free Press, 2003, p. 100.

2. Jonathan Cowan and Jim Kessler, "Changing the Gun Debate," *Blueprint Magazine,* July 12, 2001. www.ndol.org.

Chapter 1: The Gun Culture in America

3. Quoted in Geoffrey C. Ward, *The West: An Illustrated History.* Boston: Little, Brown, 1996, p. 279.

4. Alexander DeConde, *Gun Violence in America.* Boston: Northeastern University Press, 2001, p. 71.

5. Quoted in William Weir, *A Well Regulated Militia.* North Haven, CT: Archon Books, 1997, p. 72.

6. Quoted in Holly Yeager, "Two Close Calls," *Houston Chronicle,* 1997. www.chron.com.

7. Quoted in Osha Gray Davidson, *Under Fire: The NRA and the Battle for Gun Control.* New York: Henry Holt, 1993, p. 45.

8. James Jay Baker, "2002 NRA Annual Meeting Speech," NRA Institute for Legislative Action, 2002. www.nraila.org.

Chapter 2: Second Amendment Interpretations

9. Quoted in Eugene W. Hickock Jr., ed., *The Bill of Rights Original Meaning and Current Understanding.* Charlottesville: University Press of Virginia, 1991, p. 22.

10. U.S. Constitution Online, "Madison's Introduction of the Bill of Rights," www.usconstitution.net.

11. U.S. Constitution Online, "The Virginia Declaration of Rights," www.usconstitution.net.

12. Quoted in Sanford Levinson, "The Embarrassing Second Amendment," *Yale Law Journal* 99, December 1989: 637–659. www.constitution.org.

13. Quoted in David Kopel, "A Right of the People," *National Review Online*. October 25, 2001. www.nationalreview.com.

14. Quoted in Reason Online, "Quotes," December 1999. www.reason.com.

Chapter 3: Different Approaches to Gun Control

15. Brady Campaign to Prevent Gun Violence, "The Brady Law: Preventing Crime and Saving Lives." www.bradycampaign.com.

16. *Virginian-Pilot,* "A Deadly Loophole Needs Closing in Va.," January 12, 2003, p. J2.

17. Wayne LaPierre, *Guns, Crime, and Freedom.* Washington, DC: Regnery Publishing, 1994, p. 43.

18. Josh Sugarmann, *Every Handgun Is Aimed at You: The Case for Banning Handguns.* New York: New Press, 2001, p. 177.

19. James Jay Baker, "For the Record—Speech at the 2000 NRA Convention," NRA Institute for Legislative Action, June 6, 2001. www.nraila.org.

20. John R. Lott Jr., "Bullets and Bunken: The Futility of 'Ballistic Fingerprinting,'" *National Review,* vol. 54, no. 21, November 11, 2002. http://pqasb.pqarchiver.com.

21. David Hemenway, Ph.D., "Regulation of Firearms," *New England Journal of Medicine* 339, no. 12, September 17, 1998. www.vahv.org.

Chapter 4: Guns and Kids

22. Join Together Online, "Death of Policeman's Child Shows Importance of Securing Guns," February 4, 2003. www.join together.org.

23. 4-H Shooting Sports, "Kids 'n' Guns." www.4-hshooting sports.org.

24. Quoted in Margie Fishman, "Promising to Behave—In Writing." www.newsday.com.

25. United Methodist News Service, "Teens Fight Against Violent Video Games Builds Steam," March 5, 2001. http://umns. umc.org.

Chapter 5: Can Gun Violence Be Reduced Without Gun Control?

26. Quoted in Matthew Mock, "Despair Fills Md. Gun Dealers," *Washington Post,* December 31, 2002, p. A01. www.washington post.com.

27. Quoted in *Frederick News-Post,* "Gun Laws Start Today," January 1, 2003, p. A-1.

28. Quoted in Chris Cox, "One Big Victory, Now Another Big Battle," NRA Institute for Legislative Action, May 15, 2003. www.nraila.org.

29. Quoted in Dick Dahl, "New Research 'Shoots Down' Concealed-Carry Claims," Join Together Online, November 11, 2002. www.jointogether.org.

Glossary

assault weapon: Selective-fire firearms that are capable of fully automatic, semiautomatic, or burst fire.

automatic firearm: A firearm that fires cartridges as long as both the trigger is depressed and there are cartridges available in the feeding system.

background check: An investigation of a gun purchaser's background through the state police or the FBI's NICS to determine if the purchaser is prohibited from buying a gun.

ballistic fingerprint: The unique marking a gun leaves on a bullet after a bullet has been fired from the gun.

Brady law: A federal law that requires federally licensed dealers to perform background checks on gun purchasers.

carbine: A lightweight, short-barreled, repeating rifle.

Child Access Protection (CAP) laws: Laws that require adults either to store loaded guns in a place where children reasonably cannot get to them or to use a device to lock the gun so children cannot access them.

concealed carry weapon (CCW): A weapon that a person carries hidden from view.

federal firearm license (FFL): A license issued by the U.S. government allowing a person to sell firearms. All persons who sell firearms as part of their business require this license.

gun control: Government regulations of the manufacturing, buying, selling, and use of firearms.

gun license: A certificate that certain state governments require in order for a person to own a gun. The certificate is issued only if the individual has met certain requirements, such as passing an extensive background check or proving firearm safety knowledge, as required by the state.

gun registration: An official record of the transfer of a gun from one owner to another. Currently not required in the United States.

gun rights: The right of individuals to bear and use arms.

gun show loophole: A way for gun purchasers to obtain firearms at a gun show without undergoing a background check by purchasing guns from dealers who are unlicensed and not subject to the Brady law.

handgun: A firearm designed to be held and fired with a single hand, such as a pistol or a revolver.

lobbying: Attempting to persuade members of the government's legislature or legislative committees to approve, modify, or reject proposed legislation.

National Instant Criminal Background Check System (NICS): An FBI electronic database of criminal records. Gun vendors call this database to check a person's background to ensure that the person is legally allowed to purchase a firearm.

Saturday night specials: Cheap, easily concealable handguns.

semiautomatic firearms: A firearm designed to fire a single cartridge and to reload the chamber each time the trigger is pulled.

trigger locks: Lock mechanisms that are placed on guns so that a person must either have a key or know the combination to open the lock before using the gun.

unlicensed dealer: A dealer who does not require a federal license from the government to sell firearms because the dealer does not sell guns as part of a business, but sells from the dealer's private collection of firearms.

waiting period: The amount of time a person must wait between purchasing a gun and receiving the gun.

Organizations
to Contact

The following organizations are involved in gun violence issues and gun control issues. They address the scope of gun violence, the pros and cons of gun control measures, alternative solutions to gun violence, and other topics related to the gun control debate.

Brady Campaign to Prevent Gun Violence
1225 Eye St. NW, Suite 1100
Washington, DC 20005
(202) 898-0792
fax: (202) 371-9615
www.bradycampaign.com

This citizen lobby works for stricter regulation of the sales and ownership of firearms through federal and state legislation. The lobby provides citizens with information about gun campaigns and how they can contact their legislators to voice their opinions about such campaigns. This organization promoted the successful passage of the Brady Bill, which mandates background checks of firearm purchasers by federally licensed dealers.

Brady Center to Prevent Gun Violence
1225 Eye St. NW, Suite 1100
Washington, DC 20005
(202) 289-7319
fax: (202) 408-1851
www.bradycenter.org, www.gunlawsuits.org

The center is an educational outreach organization dedicated to reducing gun violence, and it's a sister organization of the Brady Campaign to Prevent Gun Violence. Its Legal Action Project provides free representation to gun violence victims against gun manufacturers and provides citizens updates on gun lawsuits through its website.

Bureau of Alcohol, Tobacco, Firearms, and Explosives (ATF)
U.S. Department of Justice
Office of Public and Governmental Affairs
650 Massachusetts Ave. NW, Room 8290
Washington, DC 20226
(202) 927-7770 (Firearms Programs Division)
e-mail: atfmail@atf.gov
www.atf.treas.gov

This bureau's responsibilities are to reduce violent crime and protect the American public. The ATF enforces federal laws and regulations relating to alcohol, tobacco, firearms, explosives, and arson. It produces publications such as *Gun Crime Trace Reports, Firearms Commerce in the United States,* and *Federal Firearms Regulations Reference Guide.* Its website contains facts and studies concerning youth crime, firearm violence, and firearm regulations.

Centers for Disease Control and Prevention (CDC)
1600 Clifton Rd.
Atlanta, GA 30333
(404) 639-3311
e-mail: ohcinfo@cdc.gov
www.cdc.gov

As a leading federal agency for protecting the health and safety of people, the CDC plays a key role in coordinating activities and programs to prevent firearm-related injuries. Additionally, along with the Consumer Product Safety Commission, in 1992 it established a nationwide system to track firearm-related injuries, the National Electronic Injury Surveillance System (NEISS), which collects data on firearm-related injuries from a population-based sample of ninety-one hospitals. Articles such as "Firearm-Related Injury Surveillance" from the *American Journal of Preventative Medicine* can be ordered on its website at no cost.

Coalition to Stop Gun Violence (CSGV)
1023 15th St. NW, Suite 600
Washington, DC 20005

(202) 408-0061

www.csgv.org

The CSGV's mission is to stop gun violence by fostering effective community and national action. It lobbies for federal and state laws that would require handgun licensing and handgun registration, and it supports a ban on the importation, manufacture, sale, and transfer of handguns and assault weapons, with certain exceptions such as the police and military. Its website provides updates on both state and federal gun legislation.

Co/Motion

Alliance for Justice

11 Dupont Circle NW

2nd Floor

Washington, DC 20036

(202) 822-6070

www.comotionmakers.org

Co/Motion is a national program that helps organizations throughout the country foster youth leadership. The program accomplishes this by providing assistance in the design and implementation of youth programs that address community problems. The Co/Motion Youth Gun Violence Prevention Initiative specifically assists organizations with youth programs that address the gun violence problem. Examples of Co/Motion assistance provided for gun violence prevention programs include training youth how to design and run projects, providing grants for projects, and providing ongoing technical assistance during implementation of the projects.

Independence Institute

14142 Denver West Pkwy., Suite 101

Golden, CO 80401

(303) 279-6536

e-mail: independenceinstitute@i2i.org

www.i2i.org

The Independence Institute is a nonpartisan, nonprofit public policy research organization dedicated to providing information to citizens about public policy issues. It favors gun rights and it publishes papers arguing against gun control. Its website contains several articles and links to books that discuss the Second Amendment and gun control issues.

Join Together Online
One Appleton St., 4th Floor
Boston, MA 02116-5223
(617) 437-1500
e-mail: info@jointogether.org
www.jointogether.org

Join Together is a project of Boston University School of Public Health and is an online resource supporting those who are working against substance abuse and gun violence. It provides a free daily update to e-mail subscribers about gun violence and substance abuse–related news.

National Rifle Association (NRA)
NRA Development Office
11250 Waples Mill Rd.
Fairfax, VA 22030
(703) 267-1130
www.nra.org

This association is the largest American organization of gun owners, with over 4 million members. Since its inception, the NRA has provided firearms education to people throughout the United States. A major proponent of gun rights, the NRA lobbies against gun control laws, believing that these laws violate the Second Amendment. The NRA publishes monthly magazines, such as the *American Rifleman* and *American Hunter,* in addition to books, pamphlets, and reports on gun ownership, gun rights, and gun safety.

Project Safe Neighborhoods
Office of Justice Programs
810 7th St. NW
Washington, DC 20531
e-mail: info@projectsafeneighborhoods.gov
www.psn.gov

Project Safe Neighborhoods, part of the U.S. Office of Justice Programs, is led by the U.S. attorney general and is committed to reducing gun crime in America by providing local programs that target gun crime with tools necessary to be successful, such as funding to hire more prosecutors and training for state and local law enforcement. It seeks to achieve coordination between federal, state, and local law enforcement, with an emphasis on intelligence gathering, aggressive prosecutions, and account-ability through performance measures. Its website provides detailed information about the program, gun crime news, and ways Americans can reduce gun violence in their neighbor-hoods.

Second Amendment Foundation
12500 NE 10th Pl.
Bellevue, WA 98005
(425) 454-7012
e-mail: info@saf.org
www.saf.org

This foundation is dedicated to educating Americans about the Second Amendment and their right to keep and bear firearms. It is a proponent of gun rights and believes that gun control laws violate the Second Amendment. The foundation provides infor-mation about the amendment through publications, such as *Gun Week,* published thirty-six times per year, and *Women & Guns,* a monthly magazine.

Second Amendment Sisters
900 RR 620 S.
Suite C101, PMB 228
Lakeway, TX 78734
Phone/Fax: (877) 271-6216
www.2asisters.org

The Second Amendment Sisters is a pro–gun rights women advocacy group dedicated to preserving the right of self-defense. It provides education about the Second Amendment and gun ownership to the public through programs. Its website provides suggested articles, books, and Internet links for more information about gun ownership, gun control, and the Second Amendment.

Violence Policy Center (VPC)
1140 19th St. NW, Suite 600
Washington, DC 20036

e-mail: info@vpc.org
www.vpc.org

The Violence Policy Center is an educational foundation that conducts research on violence in America, examines the role of firearms in America, and explores ways to decrease firearm-related death and injury through developing violence reduction policies and proposals. In an effort to educate the public about firearm violence, each year the VPC releases several studies on a broad spectrum of gun violence issues, including *Kids in the Line of Fire: Children, Handguns, and Homicide; Start 'Em Young: Recruitment of Kids to the Gun Culture;* and *"Officer Down"—Assault Weapons and the War on Law Enforcement.*

For Further Reading

Books

Helen Cothran, ed., *Gun Violence: Opposing Viewpoints.* San Diego: Greenhaven Press, 2003. Through articles written by people on both sides of the gun control debate, this book presents different viewpoints on gun violence and gun control issues. Among the issues addressed are the Second Amendment, gun control effectiveness, and causes of gun violence.

Kim H. Henny, ed., *Guns and Violence: Current Controversies.* San Diego: Greenhaven Press, 1999. This book presents a variety of opinions about gun control and gun rights issues, taken from articles and book excerpts written by experts in the field.

Jeffrey Ferro, *Gun Control: Restricting Rights or Protecting People? (Information Plus Reference Series).* Wylie, TX: Information Plus, 2001. This succinct and easy-to-read book provides a history of the United States' gun culture and current information regarding today's gun control debate. Topics include America's gun culture, current gun laws, and public opinion regarding gun control.

JoAnn Bren Guersey, *Youth Violence: An American Epidemic?* Minneapolis, MN: Lerner, 1996. This book examines violence among American youth and addresses topics such as gang violence, violence at school, and use of firearms among youths.

Websites

Common Sense About Kids and Guns (www.kidsand guns.org). This public education program provides information on how to prevent children from being affected by gun violence. Its user-friendly website offers statistics and facts about children and gun violence, and a list of Internet resources covering many topics, including safe gun storage and what kids can do to prevent violence.

Gun Violence, Live by the Gun, Die by the Gun
(www.pbs.org). This Internet resource, sponsored by PBS, summarizes and provides a transcript of the "Gun Violence: Live by the Gun, Die by the Gun" episode from *In the Mix,* a PBS weekly show that discusses issues affecting the world today. It includes interviews with several young adults about their experiences with guns. Additionally, this website includes youth gun statistics and an opportunity for young adults to voice their own opinions about guns.

Works Consulted

Books

Peter Harry Brown and Daniel G. Abel, *Outgunned: Up Against the NRA*. New York: Free Press, 2003. The authors, who support gun control, examine the NRA's efforts to protect firearm manufacturers from lawsuits and to prevent gun control proposals from becoming laws.

Osha Gray Davidson, *Under Fire: The NRA and the Battle for Gun Control*. New York: Henry Holt, 1993. The author presents a balanced view of the NRA's history, its positions on gun rights and gun control issues, and its influence on American politicians.

Alexander DeConde, *Gun Violence in America*. Boston: Northeastern University Press, 2001. This book details the history of America's gun culture and how gun control became a significant issue. The author studies the modern debate, examining the key players and their positions.

Eugene W. Hickock Jr., ed., *The Bill of Rights Original Meaning and Current Understanding*. Charlottesville: University Press of Virginia, 1991. This book explores the meaning and intent of each of the Bill of Rights amendments.

Gary Kleck and Don B. Kates, *Armed: New Perspectives on Gun Control*. Amherst, NY: Prometheus Books, 2001. In this book, the authors examine the various positions in the gun control debate, and draw pro–gun rights conclusions, based on their own experiences and research, along with studies and statistics that they have examined.

Wayne LaPierre, *Guns, Crime, and Freedom*. Washington, DC: Regnery Publishing, 1994. The author, with a long history of leadership positions within the NRA, defends private gun ownership and argues against gun control. He concludes that a tough judicial system and teaching gun safety are the best methods to reduce gun violence in the United States.

Lee Nisbet, PhD, ed., *The Gun Control Debate: You Decide.* Amherst, NY: Prometheus Books, 2001. In this collection of articles and studies, experts offer different opinions on all aspects of gun control, from America's gun culture to whether gun control is effective at reducing gun violence.

Josh Sugarmann, *Every Handgun Is Aimed at You: The Case for Banning Handguns.* New York: New Press, 2001. The author presents statistics, studies, and gun violence incidents to support his position that handguns should be banned.

Geoffrey C. Ward, *The West: An Illustrated History.* Boston: Little, Brown, 1996. This book discusses life in the West during the 1800s, including the use of revolvers and rifles.

William Weir, *A Well Regulated Militia.* North Haven, CT: Archon Books, 1997. The author, a member of both the Brady Campaign to Prevent Gun Violence and the NRA, presents a balanced look at the history of America's gun culture and today's gun control debate. He explores the meaning of the Second Amendment, court cases regarding the Second Amendment, and current positions of both sides of the debate.

Periodicals

Economist, "From the Hip," November 23, 2002.

Frederick News-Post, "Gun Laws Start Today," January 1, 2003.

Robin M. Ikeda, M.D., James A. Mercy, Ph.D., and Stephen P. Teret, M.P.H., eds., "Firearm-Related Injury Surveillance," Supplement to *American Journal of Preventive Medicine* 15, no. 3, October 1998.

Mike Knepler, "Anti-Violence Work Teaches Kids to Care," *Virginian-Pilot,* November 18, 2002.

Mark Knepler, "At City Council Meeting, Norfolk Teen to Suggest Anti-Violence Initiatives," *Virginian-Pilot,* January 28, 2003.

Christopher Lee, "Project Exile Was Not Responsible for Drops in Crime," *Virginian-Pilot,* January 5, 2003.

Collin Levey, "Liberals Have Second Thoughts on the Second Amendment," *Wall Street Journal,* November 22, 1999.

Eric Lichtblau, "Bush, NRA, Clash over Renewing Ban on Some Guns," *Virginian-Pilot,* May 8, 2003.

Newsweek, "Descent into Evil," November 4, 2002.

U.S. Department of Health and Human Services, Centers for Disease Control and Prevention, National Center for Injury Prevention and Control, *Fatal Firearm Injuries in the United States 1962–1994.* Washington, DC: U.S. Government Printing Office, 1997.

U.S. Department of Health and Human Services, Centers for Disease Control and Prevention, National Center for Injury Prevention and Control; Substance Abuse and Mental Health Services; and National Institutes of Health, National Institute of Mental Health, *Youth Violence: A Report of the Surgeon General—Executive Summary.* Washington, DC: U.S. Government Printing Office, 2001.

U.S. Department of Health and Human Services, Division of Violence Prevention, Centers for Disease Control and Prevention, National Center for Injury Prevention and Control, *Best Practices of Youth Violence Prevention: A Sourcebook for Community Action.* Washington, DC: U.S. Government Printing Office, 2002 (revision).

U.S. Department of Justice, Office of Justice Programs, Bureau of Justice Statistics, *Firearm Use by Offenders.* Washington, DC: U.S. Government Printing Office, 2001.

U.S. Department of the Treasury, Bureau of Alcohol, Tobacco, Firearms and Explosives, *Crime Gun Trace Reports (2000) National Report.* Washington, DC: U.S. Government Printing Office, July 2002.

Virginian-Pilot, "A Deadly Loophole Needs Closing in Va.," January 12, 2003.

Internet Sources

ABC News, "Violence in U.S. Schools," April 20, 1999. www.abcnews.com.

Jonathan Aiken, "Maryland School District Adds Gun Safety to Curriculum," CNN, March 6, 2001. www.cnn.com.

American Rifleman, "Armed Citizen," July 2000. www.nraila.org.

James Jay Baker, "2002 NRA Annual Meeting Speech" NRA Institute for Legislative Action, 2002. www.nraila.org.

James Jay Baker, "For the Record—Speech at the 2000 NRA Convention," NRA Institute for Legislative Action, June 6, 2001. www.nraila.org.

Mariso Bello, "Spike in Sales Defies State's Decade Long Trend," *Pittsburgh Tribune-Review,* November 3, 2002. www.pittsburghlive.com.

Jane Black, "To Keep and Bear (Licensed) Arms," *Business Week* Online, October 25, 2002. www.businessweek.com.

Boy Scouts of America, "Guide to Safe Scouting, VIII—Guns and Firearms." www.scouting.org.

Brady Campaign to Prevent Gun Violence, "The Brady Law: Preventing Crime and Saving Lives." www.brady campaign.com.

Brady Campaign to Prevent Gun Violence, "Child Access Protection (CAP) Laws and Gun Owner Responsibility Questions and Answers," February 2002. www.brady campaign.org.

Brady Center to Prevent Gun Violence, "The Second Amendment Myth and Meaning." www.gunlawsuits.org.

Bureau of Alcohol, Tobacco, Firearms and Explosives, "Brady Handgun Violence Prevention Act Questions and Answers," November 27, 1998. www.atf.treas.gov.

Mike Carter and Steve Miletich, "Gun Shop Faces Criminal Probe; Sniper Suspects Allegedly Got Rifle There," *Seattle Times,* December 4, 2002. http://seattletimes.com.

CNN, "4 Dead in Arkansas School Shooting," March 24, 1998. www.cnn.com.

CNN, "'Million Mom March' Puts Gun Control Back in Legislative Firing Line," May 15, 2000. www.cnn.com.

Colt, "History of Colt," www.colt.com.

Jonathan Cowan and Jim Kessler, "Changing the Gun Debate," *Blueprint Magazine,* July 12, 2001. www.ndol.org.

Chris Cox, "One Big Victory, Now Another Big Battle," NRA Institute for Legislative Action, May 15, 2003. www.nraila.org.

Dick Dahl, "New Research 'Shoots Down' Concealed-Carry Claims," Join Together Online, November 11, 2002. www.jointogether.org.

Gary Delsohn, "Ballistic-Fingerprint Study Triggers Dispute," *Fresno Bee,* November 19, 2002. www.fresnobee.com.

Melissa Drosnack, "Bill Would Restrict Gun Records," *Houston Chronicle,* February 12, 2003. www.chron.com.

Jonathon Dube, "Armed with Data," ABC News, March 7, 2001. www.abcnews.com.

Joan Finn, "Gun Control Group Savors Assembly Vote," *Montclair Times,* November 21, 2002. www.montclair times.com.

Margie Fishman, "Promising to Behave—In Writing." www.newsday.com.

4-H Shooting Sports, "Kids 'n' Guns." www.4-hshooting sports.org.

Hartford Courant, "First-Time Gun Permits, Sales on Rise in State," November 25, 2002. www.ctnow.com.

David Hemenway, Ph.D., "Regulation of Firearms," *New England Journal of Medicine* 339, no. 12, September 17, 1998. www.vahv.org.

International Hunter Education Association, "Hunter Education Requirements." www.ihea.com.

Join Together Online, "Ashcroft Says Project Safe Neighborhoods Reducing Gun Crimes," February 6, 2003. www.jointogether.org.

Join Together Online, "Bill Would Shut the Court House Door to Victims of Gun Violence," March 4, 2003. www.jointogether.org.

Join Together Online, "Death of Policeman's Child Shows Importance of Securing Guns," February, 4, 2003. www.join together.org.

Join Together Online, "FSA & MAC: What John Ashcroft Isn't Doing to Fight Gun Violence and Terrorism," February 3, 2003. www.jointogether.org.

Join Together Online, "Ore. High-School Student Addresses Violent Video Games," February 19, 2003. www.join together.org.

Join Together Online, "Overview—Comparison with Other Countries," www.jointogether.org.

Jonathan Karl, "NRA Reacts to Arkansas Shooting," CNN, March 25, 1998. www.cnn.com.

David Kopel, "A Right of the People," *National Review Online,* October 25, 2001. www.nationalreview.com.

Sanford Levinson, "The Embarrassing Second Amendment," *Yale Law Journal 99,* December 1989: 637–659. www. constitution.org.

John R. Lott Jr., "Bullets and Bunken: The Futility of 'Ballistic Fingerprinting,'" *National Review,* vol. 54, no. 21, November 11, 2002. www.republicandailynews.com.

John R. Lott Jr., "Some Time to Kill: In Waiting Periods, Gun Buyers Are at Mercy of Criminals." www.keepandbear arms.com.

Mark Mazzetti, "Taking a (Gun) Powder? The Gun Control Movement Gets Pragmatic," *U.S. News & World Report.* May 7, 2001. www.usnews.com.

Shannon McCaffery, "Bush Supports New Extension of Assault Weapons Ban," *Salt Lake Tribune,* April 12, 2003. www.tribaccess.com.

Patrick McShea, "Perspective: At a Gun Safety Course for Boys, Respect for Tradition Is Instilled," *Pittsburgh Post-Gazette,* October, 25, 2000. www.post-gazette.com.

A.M. Miniño, E. Arias, K.D. Kochanek, S.L. Murphy, and B.L. Smith, "Deaths: Final Data for 2000," *National Vital Statistics Reports* 50, no. 15, September 16, 2002. www.cdc.gov.

Matthew Mock, "Despair Fills Md. Gun Dealers," *Washington Post,* December 31, 2002. www.washingtonpost.com.

Pennsylvania Game Commission, "Hunter Trapper Education Program." www.pgc.state.pa.us.

David Phinney, "When Laws Take Aim at Guns," www.abc news.com.

Jane Prendergast, "Police, Feds Go After Gun Criminals," *Cincinnati Enquirer,* June 19, 2002. www.enquirer.com.

Michael R. Rand, "Guns and Crime: Handgun Victimization, Firearm Self Defense, and Firearm Theft," NCJ 147003, U.S. Department of Justice, Bureau of Justice Statistics, May 1994. www.ojp.usdoj.gov.

Reason Online, "Quotes," December 1999. www.reason.com.

Roger Rosenblatt, "The Killing of Kayla," *Time,* March 13, 2000. www.time.com.

Jerry Seper, "Ashcroft Touts Rise in Federal Gun-Crimes Prosecutions," *Washington Times,* January 31, 2003. www.washingtontimes.com.

David Sheppard, Heath Grant, Wendy Rowe, and Nancy Jacobs, "Fighting Juvenile Gun Violence," *Juvenile Justice Bulletin,* September 2000. www.ncjrs.org.

Amy Sinatra, "Building Safer Guns," ABC News. www.abc news.com.

Jeffrey Snyder, "Fighting Back: Crime, Self-Defense, and the Right to Carry a Handgun," *Cato Policy Analysis* No. 284, October 22, 1977. www.cato.org.

Thomas Sowell, "Twisted Barrel of Anti-Gun Logic," *Washington Times,* December 1, 2002. www.washington times.com.

Dalia Susson, "A Sniper Curb," ABC News, October 22, 2002. www.abcnews.com.

United Methodist News Service, "Teens Fight Against Violent Video Games Builds Steam," March 5, 2001. http://umns. umc.org.

U.S. Constitution Online, "Madison's Introduction of the Bill of Rights," www.usconstitution.net.

U.S. Constitution Online, "The Virginia Declaration of Rights," www.usconstitution.net.

U.S. Department of Justice, Bureau of Justice Statistics, "Firearm Sales Rejection Rate in 2001 Similar to Prior Years," September 22, 2002. www.ojp.usdoj.gov.

U.S. Department of Justice, Bureau of Justice Statistics, "Nation's Violent Crime Victimization Rate Falls 10 Percent," September 9, 2002. www.ojp.usdoj.gov.

U.S. Government Info/Resources, "Gun Control Timeline," September 26, 1999. http://usgovinfo.miningco.com.

Violence Policy Center, "A Brief History of Firearms Law," 1998. www.vpc.org.

Violence Policy Center, "Firearms Ownership, Concealed Carrying and Self-Defense Use," 1998. www.vpc.org.

Violence Policy Center, "Unsafe in Any Hands: Why America Needs to Ban Handguns," 2000. www.vpc.org.

Holly Yeager, "Two Close Calls," *Houston Chronicle,* 1997. www.chron.com.

Websites

Brady Campaign to Prevent Gun Violence (www.brady campaign.org). This organization provides information about current gun control issues throughout the states. Its website provides up-to-date information on gun control efforts nationwide.

Brady Center to Prevent Gun Violence (www.brady center.org, www.gunlawsuits.org). A sister organization of the Brady Campaign to Prevent Gun Violence, this organization focuses on educating the public about gun control. Through its website it provides background on gun legislation and information on ongoing lawsuits.

Co/Motion (www.comotionmakers.org). Co/Motion is a national program that helps organizations foster youth leadership in addressing community problems such as gun violence.

National Rifle Association (www.nra.org). The NRA is the largest gun owners association in the United States and its website is a resource for articles and information about gun rights.

National Rifle Association Institute of Legislative Action (www.nraila.org). The NRA ILA's mission is to lobby to prevent gun control and to promote gun rights. The website provides fact sheets, articles, and speeches on a multitude of gun control and gun rights issues.

Project Safe Neighborhoods (www.psn.gov). Project Safe Neighborhoods is a government initiative to reduce gun crime in America. The website provides information on its ongoing projects and how the community can get involved in the efforts.

Student Pledge Against Gun Violence (www.pledge.org). This is an ongoing effort to get students in the United States to pledge against using guns in conflicts. This website provides information about the pledge and how schools, organizations, and students can participate in the Day of National Concern About Young People and Gun Violence.

Index

Picture Credits

Cover photo: © Photodisc
AP/Wide World Photos, 9, 39, 59, 62, 77, 78, 80
Asay. © 1997 by Creators Syndicate, Inc. Reprinted with
   permission, 31, 46
© Nathan Benn/CORBIS, 47
© Bettmann/CORBIS, 16, 20
© Bob Daemmrich/CORBIS SYGMA, 73
Brian Fairrington/Arizona Republic, 36
Gary Hershorn/Reuters/Landov, 25
© Hulton/Archive by Getty Images, 23, 34
Chris Jouan, 43
Brandy Noon, 49, 58
© North Wind Pictures, 19, 29
© Reuters/Jim Bourg/Landov, 52
© Reuters/Larry Downing/Landov, 67
© Reuters NewMedia Inc./CORBIS, 10, 42
© Touhig Sion/CORBIS SYGMA, 64
Copyright, Tribune Media Services, Inc. All Rights
   Reserved. Reprinted with permission, 70
© Stock Montage, Inc., 14
© Les Stone/CORBIS SYGMA, 26
© Philip Wallick/CORBIS, 56

About the Author

Leanne K. Currie-McGhee has published children's articles and stories in magazines such as *Highlights for Children, Guideposts for Kids,* and *Pockets.* Before focusing on her writing career, Currie-McGhee served as an engineer in the U.S. Navy. She earned a degree in electrical engineering from Northwestern University and a master's degree in business from Florida Institute of Technology. She enjoys scuba diving, eating her husband's home-cooked meals, traveling, and chronicling her journeys on her website (www.ourlifejourney.com). She and her husband live in Norfolk, Virginia, and are expecting their first child, whom they are adopting from China in 2004. This is her first book.